Finding Aaron

a spiritual practice beyond belief

Finding Aaron

a spiritual practice beyond belief

By Cathy Jane Jensen
in collaboration with
Aaron Schaffer

Published by Mission 7255, LLC

Finding Aaron: *a spiritual practice beyond belief*
By Cathy Jane Jensen in collaboration with Aaron Schaffer.

Published by Mission 7255, LLC
ISBN: 978-0-9963646-2-1
Library of Congress Control Number: 2018912265

DISCLAIMER: All the stories in this book are true. Neither Cathy Jane Jensen nor Mission 7255, LLC shall have liability or responsibility to any person or entity with respect to any loss or damage caused, or alleged to have been caused, directly or indirectly, by the information in this book.

for the kids

Table of Contents

Prologue

*"The mysteries of existence are mysterious only to the extent that
reading and writing is mysterious to those who
have not yet learned to read and write."*
–*Rudolf Steiner*

The key to learning the mysteries of existence is death, but not yours. The teaching begins by observing and documenting what thousands of other observers have documented for thousands of years about death: it never comes alone.

The premise of *Finding Aaron:* The mysteriously strange and inexplicable happenings that come with death invite us, almost beg us, to *experience* that death is not a dead end.

This is a story of accepting these invitations that I call "opening-door events." It is our story, Aaron's and mine, and our family's, but it is also *your* story. Or at least it *could be*. It begins as it ends: **Believe nothing about death. Find out about it for yourself.** *Finding Aaron* shows you how.

A car starts spontaneously, following its owner's funeral. Three times – as if on cue for those deepest in grief. A mother begs her dead son to help her find a small, cherished item lost in a completely wild forest; green pinecones fall, loudly and precisely, and following them like breadcrumbs intentionally placed, she is led to the lost treasure.

A friend's death is dreamed on Mother's Day, as she is, unbeknownst to the dreamer, attending her mother's funeral; on the same night, five family members dream with a beloved child who has died and all five wake with the exact same message. Parents hear deceased children calling; aunts see dead nephews; uncles channel guidance for missions with the dead; and small children deliver messages to total strangers. Messages from the dead.

The peculiar nature of these opening-door events is often acknowledged, but rarely investigated. Eyebrows go up, shoulders shrug, but then, seconds later, most of us are right back to the more pressing concerns of living every day. Until the moment comes when everyday living is no longer an option. This is the day that, in the words of preeminent American mythologist and author Joseph Campbell, a spiritual hero *could be* born:

> Well, there are two types of deed. One is the physical deed; the hero who has performed a war act or a physical act of heroism saving a life, that's a hero act. Giving himself, sacrificing himself to another. And the other kind is the spiritual hero, *who has learned or found a mode of experiencing the supernormal range of human spiritual life and then came back and communicated it* [my italics].[1]

According to Campbell, there are two types of trumpet calls heralding one's high adventure of "finding or learning a mode of experiencing the supernormal range of human spiritual life." Each one of us will be summoned repeatedly, Campbell says, until the call is heeded.

Campbell himself answered the call that is felt as a deep longing to learn the mysteries of existence. By combining the arts of fearless open-minded inquiry with disciplined study, he, and many others, experienced the supernormal range of human spiritual life and they have come back and communicated what they found. Repeatedly.

The other trumpet call is a high-pitched screech. Something precious is lost or stolen. Something so precious that life is meaningless without it, and, by God, you go to get back what is rightfully yours, or you gladly die trying.

Plodding, walking, or dancing along in a "difficult" or "fine" or "oh-so-happy existence," life treasons you. It's like strolling on a bright sunny day and being stabbed through the back.

THE PHONE CALL. Friday, July 2, 2010. 8:32 p.m. Barcelona, Spain. Aaron.

My gasping, grasping, horribly overwhelming need to understand *what death means* confronted the fact that the West has no culture of death. The very words sound morbid and vulgar, impolite and improper. But only because they violate the Western taboo which wraps death in a horror beyond words because no one will talk about it. Not after the funeral.

Not caring a whit about proper grief etiquette, *Finding Aaron* challenges the death taboo killing us all, rejects thoughtlessly applied labels such as "maladjusted" and "hysterical" that come with noncompliance to rules, and insists that the effort to understand *what death means* is a cultural responsibility that must no longer be palmed off to "the grievers."

Above all else, *Finding Aaron* strives to demonstrate that: *going after those stolen by death is a method of heeding the soul's call to its high adventure of learning a mode to experience the supernormal range of human spiritual life.*

This high adventure is anything but whimsical, lighthearted fun. It is difficult, lonely, and exhausting. But then, so too is the response dictated by the taboo.

The difference is that the sustained endeavor to understand one's experiences in the supernormal range of human spiritual life is what forges spiritual heroes.

For those who heed their call, helpers arrive right on time, bearing specialized weapons for the particular hero-task at hand.

The first of mine appeared out of nowhere at Aaron's memorial service in Des Moines, Iowa, U.S.A. – and plunked a stack of books into my numb arms as she firmly stated:

"He will always be with you, you know."
"What? What did you say?" I asked.
"He'll always be with you," she repeated.
"Do you really *believe* that?" I asked.
"No," she answered. "I *know* it."

I glanced down at the books and saw something about after-life science. When I looked up, the messenger was gone, but her words remained. Out of all of the messages tossed my way, hers seemed, somehow, possibly true. And it is.

It is not that I *believe* her because I read those books (and hundreds more) to be finally convinced. Nor do I *believe* her because I joined a religious community whose *belief* in an afterlife eased *that pain*. In fact, it has nothing to do with *belief* at all.

It is that by struggling mightily to understand the *experiences* of collaboration with the dead that came with the total destruction of my world, I *know* that death is not a dead end. *Finding Aaron* is an invitation for you to *know* the same.

Those who *believe* that collaborating with the dead is forbidden by the Bible will discourage you from accepting this invitation. Remind them that *all* sacred scriptures, including those of the Western Abrahamic religions (Judaism, Christianity, and Islam) document collaboration with the dead.[i] Extensively so.

Others will try to dissuade you from reading *Finding Aaron* because they *believe* that such twaddle contradicts everything known to science. But you know what? They are mistaken.

---

[i] A small sampling: The spirit of Samuel conversed with Saul; Daniel learned secrets in visions; David received the plan of the temple from a spirit; Ezekiel, Abraham, Moses, shepherds, Paul, Ananias, Mary, Joseph – and God knows how many more – saw, heard and *collaborated* with spirits, including the spirits of those we call the dead.

Collaborating with the dead contradicts nothing but a firm *belief* in an old model, just as the 14th century "twaddle" that the sun is the center of our solar system, contradicted nothing but the firm *belief* that the "universe" spun around the earth.

Those who declare that *Finding Aaron* is "purely subjective" will tease you for being interested. They will insist that to investigate collaboration with the dead would be superstitious, uninformed, and downright silly, so sure is their *belief* that collaborating with the dead is impossible.

Remind these friends that investigating *experience that contradicts belief* is called science, although giving it such a respected label does not make it an easy thing to do. The human tendency to refuse to investigate beyond beliefs is so rampant that there is even a catchphrase for it: The Semmelweis Reflex.

Dr. Ignaz Semmelweis was deeply grieved by the fact that it was safer to give birth in the streets of mid-nineteenth-century Vienna than in one of the two medical clinics he supervised, and he was determined to discover why. The answer came, sadly enough, through the death of a friend.

Searching for his pathologist friend's cause of death, Semmelweis recognized a connection between the facts that his friend had died of "childbed fever," *and* he had cut himself with his scalpel while autopsying the body of a woman who had died of "childbed fever."

Semmelweis carefully reflected: autopsies were performed in the hospital staffed by doctors and medical students, but the midwife clinic, with a maternal death rate five times lower, was autopsy-free.

Hypothesizing that the same hands that performed autopsies were carrying some sort of invisible "cadaverous particles" to the delivery rooms, Semmelweis instituted a simple experiment of handwashing with chlorinated lime. In two months' time, the maternal death rate at said hospital dropped from 18 percent to 1 percent.

Greatly encouraged, Semmelweis researched, experimented, and documented for more than a decade. In 1861, he published his life-saving discoveries with the title: *The Etiology, Concept, and Prophylaxis of Childbed Fever.* Most of his colleagues refused to read it.

Some justified their behavior with indignant declarations that doctors are gentlemen, after all, and certainly do wash their hands. Others declared that to read his work would be to "dignify the outrageous allegation that doctors were causing death," and still others took the position that the only invisible entity capable of ending life was God, who must have his reasons.

Semmelweis was furious. He accused those who condemned his work *without reading it* of being frauds, assassins, and the makers of orphans. As women continued to die in childbirth like so many flies at a picnic, Semmelweis was mocked, ridiculed, and ostracized.

In 1865, he was tricked into entering a public asylum from which he never left. There he was severely beaten by the staff, and died of an infection two weeks later. He was 47 years old.

Semmelweis is now called the "Father of Pathology," and his handwashing nonsense is today's common sense,[i] yet investigating anything that contradicts *belief* continues to be a difficult task.

---

[i] Semmelweis' research was not in vain, thanks in good part to the relatives of pregnant women who began insisting, quite forcefully at times, that clinic staff wash their hands prior to helping with deliveries.

Rest assured that *Finding Aaron* is not an attempt to get you to believe that washing hands saves lives, let alone an attempt to get you to believe that finding your dead is possible. In fact, it is not an attempt to get you to believe anything at all.

It is simply an attempt to motivate you to **acquire for yourself** a truth that has been shouted from every corner of the planet in every wisdom tradition known to humankind from the moment shouting began …

Aaron lives, regardless of my remembering him or not. All of our loved ones who walk into death before us live in a reality far bigger than what is in our hearts, deeper than what is in our memories, and clearer than what is in our minds.

To **know** this, you must **experience** it, for it is one of the mysteries of existence that no deep truth can be known until it is experienced. *But you have to allow for the experience.*

Do not comply with the beliefs, rules, and regulations surrounding death in the West, for they are what block the *experience* that death is not a dead end.

Instead, go after your dead, for this is surely the easiest method[i] to reach the goal of every religious, spiritual, and scientific practice on the planet: acquiring the truth of our essential nature. *Finding Aaron* shows *you* how.

---

[i] Easiest method in the sense of motivation, that is. Nothing other than finding Aaron could have compelled me to extend my vision far enough to get a glimpse of eternity. Absolutely nothing.

Introducing Aaron

Aaron and I enjoyed each other's company. We laughed a lot. He arranged his life to spend half the year where I was and asked me to call him more often when we were apart. Aaron often joined the adventures of others spontaneously, never needing to be the center of attention. He made his own greeting cards, and said "Happy Hallmark Day" each Mother's Day. He told me that he loved me.

Photo of Aaron with his dog Betty, taken July 2009.

Says a friend of his, "Aaron played high school football in a red and white uniform; he was a popular kid; he had many friends; he could be top dog in any clique he wanted, yet he was kind to everyone.

He was a hard worker; he loved nature and health, and he was loyal to his family and friends. He could be quite ordinary, as American as apple pie, as they say. Sometimes he liked to just hang out, and he enjoyed concerts. It came as a surprise to me, when I first got to know him, that he also had a very deep mind."

Says another, "The only time I saw Aaron really mad was when a father was bullying his little boy. Aaron shoved that man, saying, 'How does that feel?' He was satisfied when the man clearly regretted his actions and made amends with his child. Aaron was one of those people guided by his heart. He lived his life with a clean conscience, and acted fearlessly and selflessly when it was the right thing to do, a quality that greatly endeared him to his friends."

In November of 2009, Aaron joined his wife Kandy in Barcelona Spain, and in the spring of 2010, they invited Alejo (Aaron's stepdad) and me to visit them. Alejo didn't go. I did.

During the months of April and June, Aaron and I canvassed the streets of Barcelona looking for the perfect place to start a language school like the one I had in Venezuela. He would manage it and we would all live together when I came for extended consultations. I returned home to the Andes Mountains on June 1, 2010, happy as a clam to put our ideas into action. All so nicely planned. So carefully calculated.

July 2, 2010 – Mérida, Venezuela: At 2:30 p.m., as my friend Gladys and I were preparing to watch Uruguay play Ghana in the World Cup, a friend called to say that his 12-year-old daughter, Estefania, was about to undergo emergency surgery.

Both Gladys and I became aware of a sense of foreboding. Images of a funeral played in my mind – I became afraid that Estefania was going to die. As Gladys paced with anxiety, I put a rubber band on my wrist to snap myself out of the worry and negativity. Neither of us could enjoy the soccer game.

When the phone rang four hours later and "Cathy, are you alone?" hit my ears, I *knew* that something had happened to Aaron. I could not breathe. I fell. Gladys took the phone and gave the caller Alejo's cell number, and then she told me, "Aaron is in the hospital. He's had a heart attack."

Denial came to our rescue, and Gladys and I reassured each other, "Aaron is very, very strong – he can certainly survive a heart attack – everything is going to be okay." I packed a suitcase to get to Spain, my mind full of cardiac diets and exercise routines. But no, Alejo arrived home, and all was lost.

Aaron Schaffer Jensen made his entrance into this world on Friday, November 3, 1972 at 8:31 a.m. in Des Moines, Iowa, U.S.A. The time he left his body behind is given as 8:32 p.m. on another Friday. July 2, 2010 in Barcelona, Spain.

This is 2:32 p.m. in Venezuela. At the same time that both Gladys and I felt such deep anxiety and dread, Aaron stopped in a pharmacy to get some aspirin, and there he collapsed.

The Promise

On July 8, at 2:30 in the morning, in the midst of pain beyond anything I could ever have imagined, *I was suddenly filled with immense joy* and so shocked by that fact that I recorded the feeling that somehow expressed itself in these words:

> I was surrounded by, or was being held by, or I was somehow merging with, a loving presence or with love itself. I heard in my mind, or I felt and understood for a few seconds that Aaron **is** okay. I knew – I absolutely KNEW – that all is well. I knew with total certainty that I am a good mom for Aaron; that I had never lost patience with him; that I had always heard and encouraged his ideas. That patience is my virtue and that I must be patient with myself. Somehow, I was part of love and peace.

This *knowing* evoked a promise:

> I promise you, Aaron, I will find you. No matter what. However long I must be here, I will NEVER, NEVER close the door on you. I will always be looking for you. I will find you. I will do all that I can to contact you. I will never give up. I will find you.

Back in the pain-saturated realm, I didn't know how to even begin to keep that promise. I started by laminating what I had written and carrying it with me. I read it repeatedly. I listened to my recording, over, and over, trying to recapture that fleet-footed *knowing*. Each time I listened, I marveled at the peace I could hear in my own voice.

The feeling arose that my promise to find Aaron was somehow *a mission*. I had no idea what "having a mission" meant, but each time the feeling seemed to be corroborated by an event in my everyday walk-about world, I documented it.

Corroborations of the Feeling of a Mission

Aaron's Memorial Service in Spain: Father Henry gave Aaron's service in Spanish, Catalan, and English. When speaking of God, he said, "She," "He," "It," and sometimes, **"Whatever we want to call this power that fills the universe and will help us keep in contact with Aaron."**

Aaron's Memorial Service in the U.S.A.: I remember next to nothing about this service, but I do remember the woman with the books, mentioned in the prologue. I remember her green eyes flashing and her mysterious way of appearing and disappearing.

And I remember her calm certainty that **Aaron would always be with me as she delivered my books on afterlife science.** Those books were arrows in my quiver. Weapons particularly suited to this hero journey.

Visit to Sister Luke: On my way to take care of Aaron's affairs at his home in Indiana, I stopped to see my dear friend Sister Luke. She had known Aaron since his birth; she also knew she was dying of bone cancer. As interested as I in where Aaron might be and in what "being dead" could mean, Sister Luke and I spoke all night of nothing but death.

We went to mass together the next morning. When we heard, "Turn to page **772**," I jabbed Sister Luke in the ribs. Hard. (The importance of the number will be explained later.)

The message on that page was, **"I will speak of your decrees before nobles, without being ashamed."** I told Sister Luke, "This feels like a tenet for a mission that I am supposed to do."

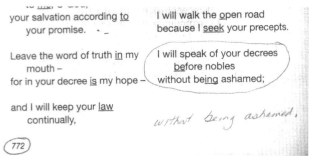

When Sister Luke made *two* copies of the message shown above (one for herself), I knew that speaking out was crucial. For the mission.

Raymond: The book *Raymond, Or Life and Death: With Examples of the Evidence for Survival of Memory and Affection After Death,* was written by a renowned physicist who had extensively investigated the after-death world into which both our sons had vanished. I felt that I needed this book, for the mission, and my sister Christy ordered it for me.

Raymond arrived with a note: "Thanks, Christy, enjoy." Signed Aaron. The signature is identical to our Aaron's signature, which is shown at top in the figure above.

Raymond is a collaboration between Second Lieutenant Raymond Lodge, who died in World War I, and his extremely well-credentialed physicist/inventor father, Sir Oliver Lodge. Together they demonstrate that it is **we, the brokenhearted, who shut the door on our dead**.

That *Raymond* found its way to our broken hearts with a signature just like Aaron's was important.[i] For the mission.

To Live Again: Looking for books on after-life science, the title of a biography caught my eye. As I took Catherine Marshall's *To Live Again* off the shelf, it fell open to the chapter title: "Is There Life After Death?" where I read:

> Some can accept immortality on faith without questioning. Others would like to believe; they hope it is true, but can get no further than hope. I, too, have had the same need of reaching beyond hope to proof. My search was made in several directions.[2]

These honest words were penned by a preacher's daughter raised in the firm *belief* of a life after death; a believer who became discouraged and confused when her inherited belief, true though it was, failed her when she needed it the most.

The words spoken at her husband's funeral, Marshall says, gained in significance for her as time went on. I recognized them, instantly, as being important for the mission:

> Let me say in a few words and in very simple words try to express what we are trying to do this morning. We are endeavoring to establish a new relationship. We have known Peter Marshall in the flesh. From now on, **we are to endeavor to know him in the spirit, and to know him in the spirit just as we have known him in the flesh** [emphasis added].

---

[i] Later I questioned my recognition of the signature – maybe it really said "Dan"? I wrote to the seller and my recognition of "Aaron" was confirmed.

Peter Marshall is still, and will continue to be, one of the ministers of this church, though no longer visible to us. The fellowship we have with him will remain unbroken, and *may God give us wisdom, grace, and strength to join hands with him*[3] [my italics].

Ergium Sanctium: On December 28, 2010, I woke up half-remembering a dream and repeating to myself the strange words, "Ergium Sanctium, Ergium Sanctium." I quickly wrote down the dream:

> There was a sort of altar, an orb or an icon or ritual. I knew it had to do with Aaron and I knew that it was something about reincarnation. I prayed, "Please show me my strong angel," like that book suggested. [I have no idea what a strong angel is, nor do I know what book I was referring to.]
>
> I saw a man about 30 years old or so with a sharp nose, slender face, with blond hair that came down a little over the ears, curly in front, and parted like bangs. Then I zoomed in on his eyes or then his eyes zoomed in on me. I kept hearing a chant: Ergium Sanctium. Ergium Sanctium.

Contacting the Classical Languages Department at the local university, I was told that *Ergium Sanctium* is Greek in origin, is connected to a medieval **alchemical** text, and is translatable as **Great and Holy Work**.

Uriel: Helpers now arrived in quick succession: Eileen, who works with angels, told me that my *strong angel* is Uriel. (I had never heard of working with angels, nor had I ever heard of an angel by the name of Uriel.) Karla, who knows a lot about many things, told me, "Archangel Uriel is working with you." (Hmm. An archangel, no less.)

I attended a workshop on *alchemy* in Elche, Spain led by Griselda, a locally recognized expert in esoteric matters.

Strangely enough, hanging on the classroom wall was a picture of Uriel with the face that came in my Ergium Sanctium dream when I asked to see my strong angel.[4] This prompted me to share my dream with the group, which prompted Griselda to introduce Uriel.

"Uriel," she said, "is the unknown archangel who works with those millions of mystics, alchemists, shamans, and seekers who endeavor to develop a direct connection with God."[i]

Having instructed me to be especially alert on Uriel's feast day,[ii] Griselda went on to claim Thomas Aquinas[iii] as the author of the medieval *alchemical text* connected to *Ergium Sanctium*.

Thomas Aquinas, she said, was the last of the great Catholic *alchemists*. He dedicated his life to searching and researching the nature of reality to acquire the truth of his Christian beliefs and he articulated his explanations for others in his Great and Holy Work, *Summa Theologiae* – hailed as one of Western Literature's most influential texts.

That it was Aquinas' **effort to acquire the truth of his beliefs that forged the direct connection with God that Uriel is said to help with** felt crucially important. For the mission.

---

[i] Uriel was de-angeled by Pope Zachary in the year 745. Perhaps he was considered a conflict of interest.

[ii] Uriel actually has two feast days: September 29 – Joe Schaffer's birthday (Aaron's biological father) and November 8 – Aaron's Grandpa Schaffer's birthday.

[iii] The feast day of Thomas Aquinas is January 28 – my birthday.

The Directory: At 2:30 in the morning, a very strong dream with Aaron woke me up. From the recording:

> Alejo said, "Cathy! Cathy! Aaron's here! He's here!" and I said, "Aarony! It's you! It's you!" He was laughing and laughing. We were all laughing and laughing. I touched his tattoo of Max, and felt his strong arms. I hugged him. He felt himself. He was laughing and laughing. We all were laughing so much. Then he told me, "Mom, I want you to work, like in a church group and **I want you to make a DIRECTORY and put in everybody's names and put them in contact with each other.** I want you to work on it and I'll come every single weekend and I'll help you work on it."

What is to be done with a dream giving such clear instructions? What is to be done with any of the opening-door events that came with Aaron's death?

- An *experiential knowing* that Aaron exists after his death brings joy and peace beyond all understanding, in the midst of pain and confusion beyond all bearing.

- *Knowing* that he still exists *evokes* a promise to Aaron that I would find him.

- The promise to find Aaron evolves into a feeling that *finding Aaron is a mission.*

- The feeling that finding Aaron is a mission is encouraged by the Spanish priest's words, "*the force that fills the universe and will help us keep in contact with Aaron.*"

- A mysterious woman declares that she does not *believe* that Aaron will always be with me, but *knows* it, as she delivers research books on *after-life science.*

- Research combines with a dream of Ergium Sanctium, archangels, and alchemy to indicate that the mission of finding Aaron is a Great and Holy Work of *acquiring the truth* that Aaron can be found.

- *Aaron collaborates* with the mission by providing instructions for *a method of accomplishment,* for this is exactly what the Directory is. As you will see.

The premise of *Finding Aaron* is that opening-door events are more than "simply messages from the dead" – they are open invitations to *experience* the truth that death is not a dead end.

Experiencing this truth is very different from, and far more important than, *believing* that life does not end with death.

Mission Statement

To motivate YOU to acquire the truth that death is not a dead end.

Acquiring transcendental truths has traditionally been called "nurturing spiritual growth." In today's parlance, it is more often referred to as "to engage in the furthering of the evolution of consciousness."

These are different ways of saying "to find or learn a mode of experiencing the supernormal range of human spiritual life." That wild range where the dead live.

With that purpose in mind, we begin with the Directory, which is both:

- A book with names listed thematically with details for contact. This begins later.

- A collection of directives providing advisory but not compulsory guidance. This begins now.

Directive 1: Wander the Wild Side of Death

"All that is gold does not glitter. Not all those who wander are lost."
–J.R.R. Tolkien

Aaron claimed *WILD*[i] on his 17th birthday by having the character Max from Maurice Sendak's *Where the Wild Things Are* tattooed on his left shoulder.

I was surprised, back then, at Aaron's choice of a hero, but have come to realize that Max deserves both recognition and emulation.

Max breaks with convention and courageously sails off to wander[ii] a wild unknown (to him) place. In spite of his belief that he was sure to confront monsters there – monsters who would like nothing better than to eat him up.

You will need that same sort of courage to wander the wild unknown (to you) place where the dead live.

---

[i] *Wild*: A natural state. Unexplored territory.
[ii] *Wander*: to walk one's own path in life.

In the words of Bohemian-Austrian poet and novelist Rainer Maria Rilke:

> This is in the end the only kind of courage that is required of us: the courage to face the strangest, most unusual, most inexplicable experiences that can meet us. The fact that people have in this sense been cowardly has done infinite harm to life; the experiences that are called apparitions, the whole so-called 'spirit world,' death, all these things that are so closely related to us, have through our daily defensiveness been so entirely pushed out of life that the senses with which we might have been able to grasp them have atrophied. To say nothing of God.[5]

The senses needed to face the strangest, the most mysterious, and the most inexplicable experiences that can meet us, may well have atrophied, but they have not disappeared. Just as an unused muscle recovers with exercise, atrophied senses recover by lowering the "daily defensiveness" that keeps eyes shut. Minds closed. Fists clenched.

Grief lowers those defenses. Abruptly. Intensely. Brusquely. A violent shortcut to the state of mind of "softened ego" sought by practitioners of meditative contemplation during long years of practice, grief allows for the face-to-face meeting of the completely unfamiliar, the strangest, and the most inexplicable experiences – like collaboration with the dead.[i]

That most of us are ill-equipped and unprepared for these meetings may well be true, but grief and a golden state of mind receptive to the miraculous are flip sides of the same coin. Tolkien is right. Not all gold glitters; some hurts. Horribly.

---

[i] In physicist James Beichler's book *To Die For: The Physical Reality of Conscious Survival*, researchers at the Laboratory for Advances in Consciousness and Health are quoted: "Throughout recorded history, claims have been made that sensitive individuals (for example mediums and **persons who have experienced the death of a loved one**) [emphasis added], can sometimes receive and share meaningful information with persons who were deceased."

This is where the road diverges. You can stay on the path worn smooth by millions of feet trudging in tune to cultural beliefs, or you can choose to wander the less explored, wild side of death, with the purpose of **seeing for yourself** if life continues. Forever.

The difficulty in exploring something that is neither sensed nor understood can be eased by the use of metaphor, such as the metaphor of electric current flowing like water in a pipe. I offer a metaphor to assist in imaging collaboration with the dead: digital computing.

Most of us have no idea how billions of (binary) bits of encoded information such as movies, photos, and songs fly over continents to land in our personal receiving devices. Not understanding *how* it happens stops no one from enjoying the fact that it does. All day, every day, everywhere.

The foundation of these modern-day marvels is the binary system of arithmetic. There is an interesting link between this epitome of "modern rational thought" (digital computing) and a 3,300-year-old Chinese text of "non-rational thought," known as the *I-Ching*[i] or *Book of Changes.* The link is Gottfried Wilhelm Leibniz.

One of the great polymaths of all times, Leibniz is credited with having invented the **binary** number system on which digital computing is based, although he would most likely say that he *perceived* it. Either way, Leibniz is the first Western mind to recognize that this most ancient of ancient *models of the great mysteries of existence* is a **binary** system.

---

[i] *The I-Ching* is commonly thought of as an oracle to be used with varying degrees of seriousness, but for those who have studied it more carefully it is thought of as much more. Terrance McKenna calls the *I-Ching* a method of exploring "outside the dimension of time." Alan Watts calls it "almost a mapping of the process of human thought," and Carl Jung calls it "a method of exploring the unconscious."

The I-Ching has 64 binary hexagrams in combinations of two characters in sets of six,[i] with each hexagram representing two sides of ONE event. When combined and decoded according to the centuries-old instructions, the hexagrams give uncannily direct answers to one's queries, as well as mysteriously useful guidance for difficult life choices.[ii]

The point to be made here is that each side of each hexagram looks to us like two separate events,[iii] most often called opposites: buy or sell; stay or go; yin or yang; birth or death. But in fact, the "two sides" always come together, *because they are one event*. Each side implies the existence of the other, because neither side can come alone. Ever.

For most of us, phrases such as *"to live in the knowledge that is beyond all opposites"* remain meaninglessly vague and beyond our ken. Leibniz is one of humanity's exceptions.

By carefully documenting patterns and hidden resonances overlooked by most, Leibniz learned *a mode of experiencing beyond rational thought*, (or in Campbell's terminology, in the supernormal range of human spiritual life) and concluded, as have many others, that what we swear is a reality made up of separate events is actually an illusionary, dream-like *fragment* of a much larger reality.

This is in perfect agreement with the sacred scriptures of the East such as Hinduism's *Bhagavad-Gita*, Buddhism's *Lotus Sutra*, and Taoism's *Tao Te Ching*. It is also in perfect agreement with the Hebrew Bible, the Christian New

---

[i] In binary mathematics, the two characters are either 0 (zero) or 1 (one). In the hexagrams, the characters are either a broken line (analogous to zero) or a solid line (analogous to one).

[ii] Jung's hypothesis for the eerily meaningful responses from the *I-Ching* is his curious principle of *synchronicity,* which is addressed in Directive 5.

[iii] This is due to the mode of experiencing that we call rational thought. Discussion continues in Directive 11.

Testament, and the Islamic Qur'an when they are understood esoterically.[i] It is also in perfect agreement with science, which has long had to postulate invisible realities acting on the visible realm in order to make sense of our everyday walk-about world.[ii]

Exploration of invisible realities, such as the electromagnetic energy that exists outside the miniscule fraction picked up by human senses,[iii] has resulted in such things as our modern conveniences, ever-increasing alternatives in the field of entertainment, and impressive advances in medical equipment.

Exploration of consciousness that exists outside the miniscule fraction rationally perceived by human minds has resulted in the discovery of modes of experiencing the supernormal range of human spiritual life, including the range where the dead live. If one human can do this, can't we all?[iv]

I can think of no stronger motivation for an investigation of death than to see for one's self if those we love more than what we call life, are alive after what we call death.

How to begin? Leibniz himself left us the answer: "It is worth noting that the notation facilitates discovery. This, in a most wonderful way, reduces the mind's labour."

---

[i] *Esoteric reading:* Sacred scriptures are *not* textbooks on history, geology, or after-death science, but instructions left by spiritual heroes whose struggle to learn the great mysteries of existence developed the insight *"to live in the knowledge that is beyond all opposites."* Compare *exoteric*.

[ii] An idea postulated by innumerable Eastern sages for centuries, as well as such eminent Western scholars as Plato, Plotinus, Augustine of Hippo, Alfred Whitehead, H. G. Wells, E. Schrödinger, and David Bohm.

[iii] The human nervous system itself is binary. A thing that fires a nerve registers as a "yes." A thing that does not fire a nerve registers as a "no."

[iv] A *very* small sampling: Elijah, Jesus, and Mohammad. Balfour Stewart, G. W. Russell, Sogyal Rinpoche, Gardner Murphy, Jack London, Krishnamurti, Aldous Huxley, Emile Cady, and William Walker Atkinson.

Directive 2: Document

*"Men occasionally stumble over the truth, but most of them pick
themselves up and hurry off as if nothing had happened."*
–Winston Churchill

Churchill was one who did not pick himself up and hurry off
when he stumbled over a truth, but saved his own life (more
than once) by heeding unseen voices, mysterious visions, and
strange intuitions. My advice is for you to do the same. And
like Churchill did, *document it all*.

While it is true that the palest ink is stronger than the best
memory, this is not the only reason for documenting.

It was by carefully noting inexplicable happenings and
baffling occurrences in his everyday-world that Leibniz
recovered his atrophied senses and accessed the non-visible
reality in which our mysterious walk-about world is
embedded.

Carry a "Walk-About Book" with you at all times. When you
stumble over any thought, feeling, hitch, glitch, or glimmer
that FEELS connected with those who have died, document it.

Have a box or a bag to stash receipts, pieces of paper, tidbits,
scribbled testimony of witnesses, and other breadcrumbs you
gather as you wander with the purpose of finding your dead.

Do not talk yourself out of documenting *every* mysterious
event, even the small ones. The time will come when you will
want to compare your experiences with similar phenomena
recorded all through time from every culture on the planet. But
you cannot do that if you don't document everything.

What follows is a smidgen from eight years, two months and
fifteen days of documenting opening-door events. For those
interested, all entries for the first year are appended.

Familiar Names Appear in Unfamiliar Ways

Orin and his brother: I was in a library and saw a small boy carrying a video. For some reason, I asked him:

"Did you find a good movie?"

"I think so," the little boy replied, handing me *The Ghost of Abu Ghraib.*

After glancing at the movie description, I told him, "This isn't good for children. What sort of movie are you looking for?"

With no hesitation whatsoever the little boy replied, "I want a movie about looking for ghosts. People don't just leave when they die. They stay and they can make the phone ring. I want to see the equipment people use to find the ghosts and how they do it."

Being interested in that sort of movie myself, we looked together. Seven-year-old Orin was chatting away when his older brother came to ask me for help in finding the book *Bones* by J. V. Smith.

I explained how the books are alphabetized by the author's last name, and we began with a random "S" shelf. Reaching the end, I asked, "What is the author's name on the very last book?"

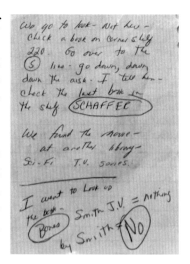

Notes from my Walk-About Book.

"**Schaffer,**" he replied.

When I heard Aaron's last name called out, a surge of energy, or a surge of something, flowed through my entire body. I had to sit down. Right there. On the floor.

The next day I went back to see about that book. The title was *Serendipity,*[i] no less.

Erin and my new Bible: I decided to investigate humanity's wisdom traditions **for myself** and thought it sensible to begin with a scripture that I knew at least a little bit about, the New Testament. I researched translations with no specific ties to any one church and with all *interpolations*[ii] clearly marked.

With my research notes in hand, I entered the BIBLE SUPER STORE.

---

[i] *Serendipity*: Discoveries made by accident and sagacity. *Sagacity*: from a Latin verb meaning to perceive keenly, related to the Latin adjective *sagus* (meaning *prophetic*), thought to be the ancestor of the English verb *to seek*. A serendipitous encounter, indeed.

[ii] *Interpolate:* to change a text by inserting material. I was surprised to learn that interpolating has a long history in Bible translations. In the King James Standard Bible, for example, *italics* do not indicate emphasis as I had always assumed, but *interpolations*, i.e., changes to the original texts.

To mention only one: In John, Chapter 10, verses 34 to 36, Jesus wonders why he is accused of being a blasphemer (which carried the death penalty) for having said, "I and the Father are one." Jesus puts his defense as:

Is it not written in your law, I said Ye are Gods? If he called them Gods unto whom the word of God came, and the scripture cannot be broken: Say ye of him, whom the Father hath sanctified, and sent into the world, Thou blasphemest; because I said, I am *the* Son of God?

In the original text, there is no article, which meant the indefinite article "a." Jesus was originally quoted as having said, "I am *a* son of God." The translators *changed the text* by adding *the*. Believing Jesus to be "*the* only begotten son of God" is, no doubt, what the *translators believed*, but it is not what Jesus is quoted as having said.

A clerk there suggested that a good way to see which translation feels right is to compare the same verse in many bibles. I answered by weeping that my son had died.

A young clerk approached me, and, ever-so-gently, she handed me a note saying, "My favorite verse in the Bible is John 11:35, and I thought it might comfort you. When a friend of his died, even Jesus cried, he was so sad. I have thought about that a lot. It is so sad when someone we love

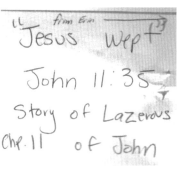

dies, that even Jesus, knowing what he knew, cried. I am so sorry. It is so sad." She hugged me with kindness. With understanding. With love.

Time passed. I chose my Bible and arrived at the counter just in time to hear a customer ask the loving young woman, "What is your name?" **"Erin,"** she replied. **CLICK. I felt it.**

Alone in Aaron's car, I closed my eyes, inhaled deeply, and asked for a message. Passing my fingers over the 558 pages of my new Bible, I opened my eyes to read my message: *The dead and the living will be fitted for immortality.*

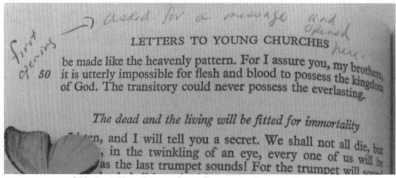

Click. The *knowing* flowed through me.

The Mystery of Asking and Receiving

Dear Mama: November 18, 2010. One year ago today, Aaron headed off on his adventure to Spain. I had been so happy and excited for him and now, here I was, beyond myself, pleading and begging with him to send me a message.

Then a strange thing happened. The top half of my body slowly became paralyzed.[i] I thought I was having a heart attack and for a long time I was on the floor thinking, "So, dying feels like this." The idea seemed lovely. It was not frightening, nor painful – only strange.

When I was able to move, I went to Aaron's car for comfort. I started it and, for some reason, I switched on the radio.[ii] There was a song playing and I heard words about a womb, and "mama" and love and laughing too loud when drinking too much wine. I was immediately alert. The announcer said, "And that was *Dear Mama* by Eric Andersen." I stayed in the car for a long time. No other song or singer was announced.

Dear Mama is from the album *You Can't Relive the Past*, dedicated to friends and family members who have died. I got my message. You see that, right?

Kandy's Grandma Carmen: Kandy called from Spain to tell me that her grandma Carmen was dying, and that Krezia (Kandy's sister) had just whispered into their grandma's ear, "Find Aaron and have him send a message that Kandy and Cathy can recognize as *being for both of them at once.*" Kandy's Grandma Carmen died that night.

---

[i] Much later, I learned that upper body paralysis is a common occurrence at the beginning of "out of body experiences."

[ii] This was totally out of character. I could not stand any noise – not from crowds, radios, television, or from any movies that were not about life after death.

The next morning I had a very strong feeling that Kandy was going to call. I told myself that it was far more likely that she would be sleeping after a very long night, but, the feeling stayed and I took the phone into the shower with me, where it did ring. A voice answered my hello with …

"Kandy? Is that you?"

"What? What did you say?" I stammered.

"I would like to talk to Kandy. Is she there? No. Wait. Sorry. I mean CATHY. Sorry. I was also looking at an e-mail. *It's like I was talking to two people at once.*"

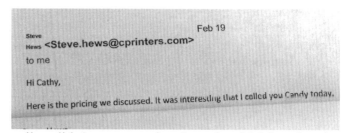

The caller didn't say much when I told him that he was collaborating with the dead, but he did write, "It was interesting that I called you Candy today." Interesting indeed.

Strange Glitches in the World of Matter

Pinecones and the fishing reel handle: Our nephew, Nick Mantle, invited Alejo and me to spend a few days healing in a wild forest. Fishing, trees, and stars – this was Nick's game plan, and we went, grateful for his kindness and love.

Once camp was set up, Alejo and I went to find our fishing spots. My reel handle was missing its bolt, so I was casting very cautiously, putting the handle in my pocket each time. When Nick called us for supper, Alejo and I made our way back to camp through tall grasses and over fallen trees.

WILD the area was, and so very peaceful. For the second time since Aaron DIED, I did not scream myself to sleep.

The next morning, Alejo was getting our fishing poles ready, and he asked me, "Cathy, where's the handle to your reel?" I had lost it, after all. Losing that handle got all mixed up with "losing Aaron," and I fell into an anguish so deep that I could not breathe.

I did not deserve such a loving son; I had not taken good care of him; I had left him alone in Iowa so that I could live in Venezuela when he was only 19 years old. If I had stayed longer in Spain, as he had asked me to, I could have convinced him to go to a doctor and he would still be here. Everything was all my fault and I couldn't bear it. I wanted to die.

I begged Aaron to help me find the handle, ignoring Alejo's protests that I was being unfair – to Aaron. "It's impossible to find that handle here," Alejo said. "Don't torture yourself."

But, I had no choice really. Somehow, finding that tiny handle lost in a wild forest symbolized finding Aaron in God knows where – and no one was going to stop me from trying.

I walked toward my fishing spot, eyes glued to the ground. Suddenly, there was a thundering CRASH! A few seconds later – another CRASH! I said aloud, "Is that you, Aaron?" and answered myself with "God, Cathy – you are so pathetic."

At that moment there was another thunderous CRASH! It was LOUD, as if things were echoing. I spun around to see a pinecone falling and I heard it POUND the earth. I searched around the trunk of the tree it had fallen from but found nothing.

I plodded on to Horseshoe Creek, wondering if a person really could drown in a cup of water.

Then, a thought came to me: "Hey, that pinecone fell *away* from the tree. Over there."

 I walked to where I had seen the fourth pinecone fall. I found it. Two steps ahead I saw another green pinecone, and two steps ahead of it – another. I took two more steps, and there was the first pinecone, **ON TOP OF THE FISHING REEL HANDLE**. I screamed, "I have had a miracle! I have had a miracle!" Nick came running over and we searched the area thoroughly. We found no other green pinecones, only those four.

I wonder, could a disinterested squirrel scamper or four lucky gusts of wind "cause" four green pinecones to crash (with a noise like the felling of a tree) in the exact formation needed for me to "luckily" find that handle?

Or could it be that, somehow, Aaron replied to my desperate pleas for help, and "caused" those pinecones to fall in the exact formation needed so that when "the thought got in," I would be led to that tiny handle, so lost in such a wild forest?

Ana and the candle: Waking up, Alejo asked me, "Is there an Ana in your family? I dreamed with an Ana with a cape down over her shoulders – sort of like what nurses wore in the past." "No," I told him, "I can't think of any Ana in my family."

Alejo got up, and then called for me to come quickly. Pointing to a lit candle, he told me that last night he had tried to use this very candle as a cigarette lighter, but it wouldn't light. Not even after he had carefully cleaned all around the wick. And now, right in front of him, the same candle he had (unsuccessfully) worked so diligently to light the night before, burst into flame. Right in front of him. But, that's not all.

I do have an Anna in my family, and I knew her story well; I just had not recognized her because she is usually called "Grandma's mom."

Eleven-year-old Anna Johnson had left Sweden to reach Clinton, Iowa on a Fourth of July. As a child, I laughed each time I heard how thrilled she was with the fireworks she thought her father had arranged for his family's arrival.

And, knowing what he was going to be told, I was saddened each time I imagined this distant grandfather running to greet his family and hold the baby who was born after his departure. I wonder what words could have possibly been used to tell him that baby Hulda had died the month before the trip.

And I wonder what words could have possibly consoled Anna's mother, Ingrid, so crippled by her grief at having, in her mind, abandoned her baby to her lonely grave in Sweden, that she refused to speak one word of English. Ever.

Label from the St. Ana candle.

And I wonder at the mystery that so tenderly weaves these long-dead family members into Aaron's Family Mission by a dream with "Anna wearing a cape-like thing," and a Santa Ana candle that spontaneously burst into flame, right in front of the dreamer.[i]

---

[i] Let that sink in: the candle burst into flame *spontaneously*. That "cannot happen," but it did.

Aaron's car starts spontaneously: After Aaron's funeral in Des Moines, many of us stayed at his Grandma JoAnn Schaffer's house. On August 2, as I was coming out of the back door, Aaron's car, parked in his grandma's driveway, suddenly started. By itself. Alone. Spontaneously.

Alejo and I both jumped. Aaron's keys were in Alejo's pocket and we figured that by jostling them, he had accidently activated a remote starter. Alejo got into Aaron's car, inserted the key into the ignition, moved it to the "on position," and then turned the car off.

When Kandy came out of the house, Alejo showed her the remote starter. He aimed the fob at the car, pushed the two buttons, and CLICK, the car started right up. Then Christy came out, and Alejo gave her the demonstration. He aimed the fob at the car and he pushed the two buttons. CLICK, the car started right up. Again. Four of us witnessed this.

That evening, family gathered to say goodbye to Kandy, who was going back to Spain the next day. When Alejo related the accidental discovery of the remote starter, Aaron's Aunt Debbie, who works at her brother's shop where they install remote starters, asked to see the fob. "There is no remote starter on his fob," Debbie said. "Only buttons to lock and unlock the doors." She seemed very sure.

Three weeks later, Alejo and I took the car to a Land Rover dealership in Des Moines to ready it for a long drive to my sister Ellen's in Washington. The car was fine, the trip uneventful. Mechanically speaking.

One month later, a group of us were on Ellen's front porch when Alejo said, "Weird – this fob is vibrating. Hey you guys! Aaron has a remote starter." Alejo aimed the fob at the car and pushed the two buttons for the first time since August 2. This time, however, the car didn't start.

We supposed that the fob needed a new battery, but then … I read about a father's truck starting spontaneously while his daughter was at his graveside. We replaced the fob battery. Nothing. Then we wondered if the remote starter had been disconnected during the maintenance check before the trip.

The first thing I did when we returned to Des Moines was to take the car back to the dealership. Aaron's Aunt Kim showed up unexpectedly, saying that she was there as a witness. We told the service manager only that, apparently, they had disconnected the remote starter two months earlier.

He asked for the fob with the remote starter. "The only fob we have is in the car," I told him. "That fob doesn't have a remote for the engine. Only to lock and unlock the doors," was his answer. I wept while Kim explained.

They tested the car. No faults were found. They tested the car again. The service manager reported the findings, "There is absolutely no problem what-so-ever with the wiring, the electrical system, or with anything else on this car. There is no way it could have started on its own, and certainly not with this fob. No way. It must have been a ghost." Kim's voice rose with emotion, "That's what *we* think," she replied.

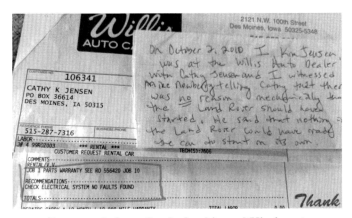

Paperwork from the dealership and Kim's note.

Aaron's car moves: For Aaron's November 3, 2010 birthday, I took his car to be detailed at a deluxe car wash. When I returned, I felt that the car was not well cleaned, and the attendant agreed to run it through again. This time there was an accident.

Apologizing, the owner said, "I am so sorry. I don't know what happened here. *I have no idea why we even started your car.* We only do that to wash the engine. Somehow, your car jumped [on the conveyor belt] and hit the car in front. *I have worked here since I was a kid and I have never seen this before.* I am so sorry. I will have to get you a new bumper."

I crumpled to the floor, sobbing that I had not taken good care of Aaron's car, just as I had not taken good care of him. Terribly upset, I told the owner that I had to leave and would return tomorrow. I called Ellen, crying, but she laughed and said, "Wow! Aaron got a new bumper for his birthday!"

The fact is that Aaron's car was in mint condition, *except* for a very slight ding in the front bumper. As it was expensive to fix, and not very noticeable, we had let it be.

"QUALITY REFLECTS IN EVERY JOB WE DO"				
CATHY JENSON 857 SOCORRA TRAIL RED FEATHER LAKES, CO 80545	Date of Loss: Year: 00 Make: RANG Model: DISCOVERY 4X4 S		CASEY'S CAR WASH	
Home: 970-881-3893 Work: Est.:	Type: UV Style: 4D UTV Engine: 8-4.0L-FI		Phone: Fax: Adjuster:	
Received: 11/11/10 Del. Date: 11/16/10 Date Paid:	Color: GREEN License: IA 429XXS Mileage: VIN: SALTL1245YA277364		Claim #: Policy: Betterment: Deductible:	

Ln.	Description	Parts	Labor Units	Team	Refin Units	Team
1 E1	FRAME		BL			
2 E1	Repair Frame assy		BL 2.00		PL 1.00	
3 E1	FRONT BUMPER		BL			

Bill to Casey's Car Wash for the bumper.

The next day, Christy went with me to the car wash. The owner was emphatic, "I am second generation at this car wash, and I have NEVER seen this happen. NEVER! *I don't know WHY we even started the car.* We only do that to wash engines. It just jumped the conveyor belt and hit the car in front of it." He agreed with Ellen, telling Christy, "I think it was her boy."

Kandy wanted to verify that the rotation of the tires could not have pushed Aaron's car into gear. So, four months later, we returned to the car wash. The owner repeatedly insisted that Kandy's rationale for the event was impossible, and he emphasized again *that he had never seen this happen in 40 years. Ever.*

"It's for sure your boy," he told me, and addressing Kandy, he asked, "That doesn't scare you, does it?" Kandy said no, but I didn't peep.

When the service manager at the Land Rover Dealership in Des Moines had said, "It must have been a ghost," I remained mute, afraid that he might be joking. When Kim replied, "That's what *we* think," I knew she wasn't joking, but I didn't ask her a thing either. Those were stumbles over a truth, but I picked myself up and hurried off, as if nothing had happened.

Facing Experiences That Are Called Apparitions

There are many terms to describe experiences of a ghostly nature: spirit, apparition, astral body, phantom, wraith, soul, shadow, presence, ghost, to name only a few. I don't know what any of these terms really mean. I only know there are so many terms because there are so many different types of experiences so well documented. A very few of our own experiences that are called apparitions follow:

Alejo's experience: At 2:30 in the morning, Alejo walked into the kitchen while I was recording the Directory Dream and told me, "I was half asleep when I heard a voice in my ear calling ALEJO! ALEJO! I thought, 'is that Cathy? Then I thought, No, there's no accent.' The voice woke me up and [with the television illuminating the room] I saw a tall, thin person sitting in the chair next to the couch with her (?) hands folded in her (?) lap. There was a peaceful feeling of calmness and quiet for about 20 seconds. Then she (?) slowly faded away."

Ellen's experience: Ellen called on October 20 (2010) to report that in the very early morning she had seen and felt a sort of presence. "A gray form," she called it. Ellen said that she asked aloud, "Aarony, is that you?" The form lingered a bit by her photos, and then went slowly down the stairs.

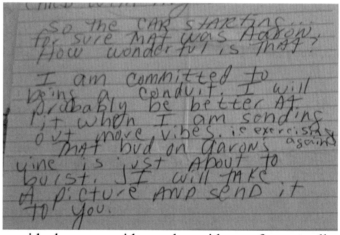

Ellen said she was wide-awake with no fear at all, and, committing to be a "conduit," she sent the letter shown above.

Kandy's experience: Kandy called, whispering, "All the doors in the apartment were closed, and I was in bed. At 1 a.m. [Aaron's usual bedtime] the door to the bedroom opened very slowly. There was no draft. I felt the bed depress and I HEARD the bed springs squeak."

Marisol's experience: Driving by a cemetery in Merida, Venezuela, my sister-in-law Marisol (Alejo's sister) saw her friend Jose casually strolling. In the cemetery. Upon sharing this with her husband Efraín, he informed her that she was most definitely mistaken. Jose was not in Merida, he said, but in a hospital in Caracas. The next day, Marisol told a group of us that she had seen Jose ambling in the same cemetery, again.

Efraín laughed at her "hallucinations." He had talked to Jose the day before, he said, and he was doing great. In fact, he would be leaving the hospital in just a couple of days. When Marisol firmly declared, "Jose is going to die," Efraín chuckled over her "crazy voodoo death stuff." Jose was buried in that cemetery four days later.

I didn't know what to make of Marisol's experience or of any of these events, and, just as Rilke warned, my "daily defensiveness" was tempted to discredit the witnesses, in spite of the fact that I was one of them. I researched instead and found innumerable, well-documented cases of just such experiences. And so will you. If you look.

Inexplicable Messengers

Efraín, *A Course in Miracles*, and the man: Efraín Rojas Oquendo is Marisol's stepson; brother to her two children; our nephew; and Aaron's cousin.

As is typical of most Venezuelans, Efraín has always been very warm and cordial. And like most of us (as far as Alejo and I knew), more concerned with material pursuits than with any spiritual endeavors.

After Aaron's death, Efraín called Alejo, saying that he wanted to share some things with him that would help me. When they met, Efraín explained that he had been working hard on spirituality for the last few years, and, among other things, he was studying *A Course in Miracles*[i] (ACIM) with a group of like-minded seekers.

Efraín told Alejo to tell me that he *knew* that Aaron was fine. This was not a belief, he emphasized, but something he *knew* through his own efforts to understand personal experiences of a mystical nature. Alejo was deeply touched.

Then, eight days later, Efrain was gone. A small airplane carrying six close friends crashed into the beautiful Andes Mountains, leaving scores of broken hearts aching in unison.

Efraín's mother Elda gave us a card from his ACIM study group, which featured the beautiful poem, *Don't Cry if You Love Me.*[ii] I took the card "as a nudge from Efraín" to finally order the book I had heard about for so many years.

A Course in Miracles has become vital in my own efforts to understand experiences of a mystical nature. On September 3, 2012, I read lessons 157 and 158. From Lesson 157:

> This day is holy, for it ushers in a new experience. You have spent long days and nights in celebrating death. Today you learn to feel the joy of life. Today it will be given you to feel a touch of Heaven, though you will return to paths of learning.

And from lesson 158, I read:

> Our concern is with **Christ's vision** [emphasis added]. Christ's vision has one law. It does not look upon a body and mistake it for the Son whom God created. **See no one as a body** [emphasis added]. Each brother whom you meet today provides another chance to let Christ's vision shine on you.

---

[i] *A Course in Miracles* is a self-study course for inner transformation.
[ii] Said to have been written by St. Augustine's mother for her son.

For some reason, I then decided to go to my school in Mérida. I had no reason to go. I had closed it for the day. But I went.

Once there, I walked to get coffee, talking to myself along the way, "Learn to see with Christ's vision – she is not a body; she is spirit – he is not a body; he is spirit – all of us are spirit," and feeling kind of nuts.

When I returned with my coffee, I found an elderly, rather disheveled, gentleman waiting patiently by the door, even though the school was obviously closed. He said that he needed to register his granddaughter.

Rather than asking him to come back when we were open, for some reason, I motioned him to follow me into the office. Once inside, all I could do was cry, "My son died. I can't do this. I want to die. I can't do this."

The man took my hand and gently said, "Profesora, come. Sit here." A small table between us, the man placed his hands on my forearms, looked straight into my eyes, and said,

"Profesora, The body doesn't matter. It is only a form for spirit to use. *Don't see anyone as a body.* Your son is right here, waiting for you to know him in spirit."

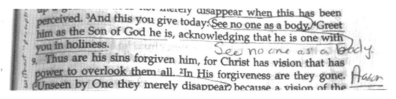

From Lesson 158 in *A Course in Miracles.*

The man continued, saying *exactly* this: "*You can learn to see with **Christ's vision** and come to know your son in his spirit.*"

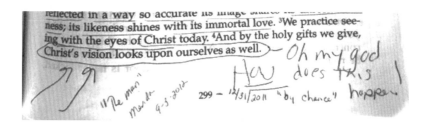

reflected in a way so accurate its image shines — ——
ness; its likeness shines with its immortal love. ³We practice seeing with the eyes of Christ today. ⁴And by the holy gifts we give,
Christ's vision looks upon ourselves as well.

Oh my god
How does this
299 – 12/31/2011 "by chance" happen!
The man mude 9-3-2012

From Lesson 158 in *A Course in Miracles*.

"Deep sorrow is not the same as love," the man told me. "And **it is love, not sorrow, that lights the way to those who have died.**"

Wonder-struck, I ran to my mother-in-law's house. I needed her perspective on "this new experience that had been ushered in – this touch of heaven" that had been given me. As I had been promised, only two hours earlier.

Love Lights the Way to thc World of Spirit

Laura Alías and Baby Jesus: My mother-in-law Laura is a member of a family with more than a little contact with Rilke's "whole so-called world of spirit."

Laura grew up hearing about the day a small light danced in front of her father all the way home from his store; how when he was telling her mother, both parents saw it hovering over the newborn baby's crib, where the tiny infant lay dead.

Laura's entire family and half the town knew that spirits walked through her Aunt Maria's living room. They also knew that Maria's daughter, Maria del Mar, talked to the dead and healed with the touch of a hand.

My mother-in-law remembered every detail of her out-of-body experience when she was seven years old, down to the embroidery on the pockets of her summer dress.

She wondered *how* she had glimpsed down into her neighbors' patios "from above," but she never doubted her experience.

For over twenty-five years, we had discussed our most inexplicable experiences with total ease. From Aaron's death onward, our only topic of conversation was dying, and what it might mean to be dead – unless others were in the room.

Other than Alejo, that is. He was no deterrent at all and more than once I heard him moaning in the kitchen, "que pesada" which means something like "she is such a drag," referring to me. But Alejo was wrong. It *has never been* a one-sided conversation.

On November 11, 2013, Señora Laura was hospitalized for a week, and when discharged, she needed 24-hour homecare. My instructions from Alejo were clear, "Say nothing about the afterlife. NOTHING! She will think that you want her to die."

Now that Laura seemed closer to death, the dictates of the taboo took over, and I spoke with my mother-in-law of superficialities and nonsense, well aware of what a coward I was.

When I finally mustered the courage to disobey the grand injunction, the two of us conspired. I reminded Señora Laura that if I died first, I would send her messages using the number 55, and she reminded me that her number is 7.

"If you do die before I do," I said, "send me something connected to Jesus, since he is like your best friend. Something clearly out of the ordinary."

"Jesus, no," she replied. **"El Niño Jesus."** (Baby Jesus.)

For more than 40 years, Señora Laura had claimed her figurine of Baby Jesus as a portal for contemplating the mysteries of existence. And so, we agreed. El Niño Jesus it would be.

On May 28, 2014, in her daughter Marisol's arms, my beloved mother-in-law left her body behind. Five weeks later, for the July 2 anniversary of Aaron's death, I was at a long-planned retreat at the Benedictine Monastery at Montserrat, Spain.

Señora Laura's having just left the physical realm added to the difficulty of claiming love, rather than sorrow, to light my way to those who have died.

In the early morning hours of July 4, I penned my own declaration of independence: I would no longer tread the conventional path of grief, paved with pain and sorrow, but would try my best to use love as my light to find those who have died.

As a symbol of my compromise to myself, I decided that, at some point during the day, I would leave my declaration and my threadbare sandals as tokens of my commitment to my new path in the special room provided in the Basilica for just these sorts of lofty promises.

Around 5 p.m., I felt compelled to call Alejo to share that I was on my way to light a candle for his mom, and would be stopping by the "room of promises" on my way.

I had been in and out of this room at least five times that very day. But this time, on the way to light my mother-in-law's candle, there was a Baby Jesus figurine exactly like hers. I was overwhelmed. I felt faint. I had to get outside.

I clutched a woman in the patio and tripped over the words gushing from my mouth. I tried to tell this total stranger about the messages from Aaron, from my dad and from my father-in-law Aniceto.

And I tried to explain the importance of the *timing* of this most recent message.

"I have been in that room at least five times today," I told the woman. "But somehow I knew to drop off the promise on the way to light her candle *now*, so that I would find her Baby Jesus."

I felt dizzy. I had to hang onto the woman's arm. She was quiet, her mind reeling, I'm sure.

Back in the basilica, I struggled to calm the emotion that comes with these types of experiences, and then I *heard* the words,[i] "All you have to do to know it is all true, Mom, is to trust your own experiences. Remember el Niño Jesus." **CLICK. Oh my GOD. I *knew*. I absolutely *knew*.**

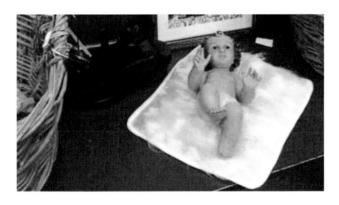

When I left the Basilica, the woman I had accosted was waiting to talk to me. Her words struck me as important and they have long stayed on my mind: "You're right," she said. "I've not seen a figurine like that for many years. How beautiful **for** your mother-in-law that you can recognize her message."

I called my sister-in-law Marisol to tell her of the event, "On July fourth I went to light a candle for your mom –" Marisol interrupted me, **"Oh, July 4. That's her Saint's Day."**

---

[i] This state of consciousness is *Hypnagogia,* which is discussed in Directive 7.

Western Rules are very clear: Grieve, as you must, but after the funeral, please grieve in the privacy of your home, or in your therapist's office. Just, please, don't grieve in public.

But ..., as Wilson Van Dusen says:

> In an ideal society, everyone would be able to see feeling and aid feeling-meaning to come forth. *Only an emotionally impaired society would leave this to hired experts* [my italics]. It should be everyone's province.[6]

In an ideal society, "non-grievers" will no longer tiptoe past the grief meetings held quietly behind closed doors in public libraries and almost clandestinely in church basements, sighing in relief they have not yet been inducted.

In an ideal society, "grievers" will no longer carry the burden of an emotionally impaired culture's determination to ignore death.

In an ideal society, everyone will know that grief resonates at the same frequency as what we so casually call love and "webs together" those people who are able to aid feeling-meaning to come forth.[i]

In an ideal society, this "webbing together" will be recognized as a method of generating a field of receptivity for opening-door events that contradict the belief that there is no communication from the dead.

In an ideal society, these opening-door events will motivate *many* to learn how to experience the wildly unexplored terrain of the dead that lies just beyond belief. That forsaken land to which we in the West thoughtlessly banish those we love.

---

[i] Like Orin in the library, Erin in the Bible store, our nephews Nick and Efraín, the man at my school, and the kind woman at Montserrat.

In an ideal society, it will be known that the type of learning needed for this experiencing is altogether different from the learning needed to navigate the web, use social media, pass exams, and get into graduate school, as this type of learning is more of an *unlearning*.

And, in an ideal society, there will be amble support and widespread encouragement for the most difficult unlearning of all: *unlearning beliefs that we don't even know that we have.*

Directive 3: Get Acquainted with your Unconscious Beliefs

"Nothing is so firmly believed as that which we least know."
–Michel de Montaigne

Getting acquainted with the unconscious beliefs running my show is *by far* the most pain-relieving step I have taken thus far. For that reason, I highly recommend the practice. It's very easy to see where to begin.

Whenever you find yourself in a firm stance of disapproval, arms crossed and mind closed, dismissing your "opponent's" experiences with, "I don't *believe* in that," you are using code for "you are challenging my (unconscious) beliefs. Back off."

It's not so easy, however, to see when you are your own adversary, busily dismissing your own life experience because you "don't believe in that." Which is exactly what I did.

In stark contrast to what many of the books I was reading seemed to say, receiving a message from Aaron did not dissolve my pain and confusion. I was on a roller-coaster ride of wonder and despair, for years.

Each time I recognized communication from Aaron, a deep peace would assure me that I would never doubt again. But I always did, and there I would be, treading water, sinking fast, head barely above the terribly quick sand – yet again.

I felt unappreciative, stupid, and dense. When I was told that messages come to those who need them the most, guilt was added to my mounting defects. I was guilty of being too sad, too blocked, too tied to Aaron's form.

I made a long list of saints, philosophers, mystics, Nobel Laureates, and geniuses who investigate(d) collaboration with the dead. I would say to myself, "These people are thousands of times smarter than I am[i] and they believe(d)[ii] in communication from the dead."

I would chant the list, under my breath, as I studied theories on the evolution of consciousness and models of how humans learn and come to know anything at all. I added more names to the list as I took notes from documentaries,[iii] read histories of science and psychology, and as I tried to understand books on physics, sacred numbers, and the illusion of time.

But no matter how much I studied and researched, no matter how I tried to convince myself, I was caught in an unbearable fluctuation between *knowing* that the communication was (somehow) from Aaron, and not understanding *how* Aaron could possibly be communicating. Until I finally did.

It was while reading Charles Tart's book, *The End of Materialism: How Evidence of the Paranormal is Bringing Science and Spirit Together,* that I became instantly aware (after such a long time) that my roller-coaster ride of peaceful certainty and desolating doubt resulted from my firmly *believing* that communication with the dead was impossible. I just didn't know it because my belief was *unconscious*. And I am not the only one so afflicted.

Those who study opinions, justified beliefs, the many processes of learning, and the many paths of acquiring a truth, state unequivocally that the *vast majority of us don't know what we most firmly believe.*

---

[i] A very small sampling: David Bohm, Abraham Maslow, Joseph Campbell, Aristotle, Plotinus, George Gurdjieff, Evelyn Underhill, Manly P. Hall, William Blake, George Russell, and Camille Flammarion.

[ii] I was wrong about this. There was no one on the list who *believed* that consciousness survives death – everyone *knew* it.

[iii] A very small sampling: *Life after Life* by Raymond Moody; *What the Bleep Do We Know* by Arntz, Chasse & Vicente; *Xico Xavier* by Filho; *Wake Up* by Jonas Elrod; and *The Living Matrix* by Becker & Massey.

We don't know our deepest beliefs, say the experts, because they are bequeathed us, like the family jewels; they are caught from our families and surrounding communities, like the flu.

In addition, continue the experts, all beliefs are composed of layer upon layer upon layer of assumptions that humans absorb, without knowing a thing about them.

And here is the kicker – we unconsciously defend our inherited beliefs with all of their unconsciously absorbed underlying assumptions. That is, humans use unconscious strategies to defend the unconscious assumptions of their unconsciously absorbed beliefs. Quite a fine kettle of fish.

In his book, Tart provides nicely worded descriptions of the "Pathologies[i] of Knowing and Learning" most commonly used for preventing unconscious beliefs from being challenged.

My favorite ruse to keep my inherited beliefs, with all of their layered assumptions, safe but not sound was:

> When human experience does not fit into material realism, for instance, there's often a specious generalization invoked to make such potentially disturbing information go away. A common method is to invoke human fallibility: people are misled, superstitious, crazy, liars, or deluded, so that you can stop paying attention to anything that doesn't fit your idea of the way the world works.[7]

What unconscious belief of mine, with its unknown underlying assumptions, was so threatened by my recognizing communication from Aaron that I denied my own experience?

---

[i] *Pathos*: to suffer. Ology: a subject of study. I suffered *pathologically* because my experiences challenged my unconscious beliefs. I had three choices: deny my experiences, pinpoint the conflicting beliefs, or give up and die.

My (unconscious) belief in the very theory that Tart mentions: material realism. And I didn't even know what it was.

On page 280 of his book, *The Self-Aware Universe: How Consciousness Creates the Material World,* Amit Goswami defines material realism as:

> A philosophy holding that there is only one material reality, that all things are made of matter (and its correlates, energy and fields), and that consciousness is an epiphenomenon of matter.

Epiphenomenon is defined on page 278 of the same book as, "A secondary phenomenon; something that exists contingent on the prior existence of something else." *Contingent* I did know, and so I understood that this *theory declares* that:

- there is ONLY a world of matter,
- thus, all things come from matter, including consciousness,
- thus, without a material brain, there is no consciousness,
- thus, there is no "survival of consciousness,"
- thus, there could be NO communication from Aaron, nor anyone else we call dead. *Not really.*

I didn't know that I believed that the theory of material realism was a fact. I only knew that *that pain* was killing me. A slow and painful suicide.

Calling myself a liar, misled and deluded, I wandered exhausted, lonely, and defeated. Victimized by myself, I badgered others to accept my evidence of communication from the dead so that I could accept it myself.

Collaboration with the dead does not contradict science. It only contradicts the *theory* of material realism with its underlying *assumption* that *the brain produces consciousness.*

To investigate evidence that contradicts this assumption is not anti-science, superstitious, naive, nor uninformed, although many who claim to be "scientific" declare that it is.

Nor is it offensive to God or against God's rules, although many who claim to be "religious"[i] declare that it is.

What is anti-science and deadly to personal/spiritual growth, is the defense of any belief system. Whether that belief system be called a scientific fact or a religious truth.

Abraham Maslow eloquently describes what happens when defense of belief gets confused with searching for truth:

> Science then can be a defense. It can be primarily a safety philosophy, a security system, a complicated way of avoiding anxiety and upsetting problems. In the extreme instance, it can be a way of avoiding life, a kind of self-cloistering. It can become in the hands of some people at least, a social institute with primarily defensive, conserving functions, ordering and stabilizing rather than discovering and renewing.

> The same is true, in my experience, for spiritual systems. They can be open-ended, error-correcting growth systems, opening to new, vital knowledge and compassion for self and others, or they can be used as a neurotic defense mechanism, protecting users from real spiritual growth while allowing them to feel superior to ordinary people and "spiritual" at the same time.[8]

Rosa Elena and Clara: Religion used as a neurotic defense mechanism just about killed my friend Clara. To understand her story you need to meet her daughter, Rosa Elena.

---

[i] The *everyday understanding* (exoteric) of humanity's sacred scriptures unconsciously endorses material realism's tenet that matter is the ground of all being. It also unconsciously endorses its (material realism) assumption that matter and spirit are different and mutually exclusive. As "nothing can be known about spirit," goes the absorbed assumption, we *must* rely on "right belief." More on this later.

Rosa Elena is a psychologist who (before I met her) had worked for many years trying to help people paralyzed by the grief of having lost someone they love.

Presenting various strategies for learning how to take the pain, how to accept the pain, how to transform the pain, how to live in spite of the pain, Rosa Elena tried to help her clients re-kindle that elusive desire to re-invest in life, blah, blah, blah – until her sister died.

Then...that sister came in spirit. Not a vague, misty, vapor-like appearance of two seconds, but a figure filled with intent and purpose. Rosa carefully documented what her sister was wearing, whom she was with, and what she said.

Two days later, her sister's child called Rosa. He was frantic. He needed her. When Rosa Elena arrived, her nephew wept; he was confused and afraid. He had seen his mom that morning, he said, and he told Rosa what his mom was wearing, whom she was with, and what she had said. His aunt opened her journal to show him the same exact experience.

And so it was that Rosa's life experiences initiated her into the higher mysteries of existence, as so often *could* happen.

Researching beyond the narrow confines of material realism, Rosa enrolled in classes, took seminars, and flocked with like-minded colleagues, all the while documenting and investigating the mysterious events that were now coming out of nowhere and from everywhere.

By the time Rosa Elena came into my life, the feeling of absolute joy that surrounded her was a powerful incentive to *learn* what she *knew*.

Each time I fretted (and I fretted a lot) that my grief might be "holding Aaron here," Rosa would throw her head back and laugh, "HA! As if you could hold Aaron anywhere. Cathy, don't you see how crazy that is?"

When I worried (and I worried a lot) that my terrible grief was somehow hurting Aaron, Rosa would tell me, "Grief is contrary to spirit – it is a cultural response based on a terrible misunderstanding. Aaron is fine. There is no way that you can hurt *him*. Your grief is only hurting *you*."

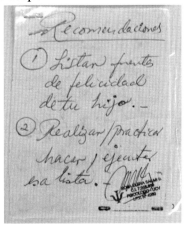

Rosa Elena gave me a prescription, but not for anti-depressants or more sleeping pills. I was to make a list of activities that Aaron likes to do and then go do them, every day, knowing that Aaron would be with me.

Rosa Elena's prescription.

Rosa had previously done all that she could to convince her clients that life was still worth living in spite of the fact that the dearest of their dear had gone. Now she does everything she can to get her clients to investigate, *for themselves,* the possibility that "the dead" are not gone, but are here, and waiting to develop a relationship in spirit. A much more difficult proposition, Rosa says.

So difficult in fact, that her own mother, Clara, could not consider it for a very long time. But not because she believed communication with the dead was impossible; Clara believed that it was wrong.

Clara belonged to a church headed by a pastor who was scared to death of death. Firm in his belief that communication with the dead could be nothing but devilish shenanigans, he forbade his flock to *investigate for themselves* the spirit communication so well documented in the very Bible he was thumping. Clara was having the same sort of trouble that Galileo had encountered long ago when "spiritual leaders" confused belief with truth. His reasoning rings true:

> I do not feel obliged to believe that the same God who has endowed us with sense, reason, and intellect has intended us to forgo their use.

Galileo's "adversaries," were knee-deep in their inherited belief that the Bible is God's explanation of the material world and so firm in their conviction that *to wonder was offensive to God* that they refused to take a better look at creation through a telescope. Galileo wrote to his friend:

> My dear Kepler, I wish that we might laugh at the remarkable stupidity of the common herd. What do you have to say about the principal philosophers of this academy who are filled with the stubbornness of an asp and do not want to look at either the planets, the moon or the telescope, even though I have freely and deliberately offered them the opportunity a thousand times? Truly, just as the asp stops it ears, so do these philosophers shut their eyes to the light of truth.

Clara finally did go beyond *the beliefs of her pastor* to investigate spirit communication for herself, and, when I met her, she was no longer relying on right belief, but on wonder.

Belief is so sure of *what is and what cannot be* that there is little room left for wonder. But it is fearless, open-minded wonder that facilitates access to the deeper dimensions of Life. As it always has.

Directive 4: Wonder

"What we lack is not a will to believe, but a will to wonder."
–Rabbi Abraham Joshua Heschel

This event begins with a member of the clergy who, in stark contrast to Clara's pastor, proposes that collaboration with the dead is not only vital to religion,[i] but the essence of the message of Jesus. The event takes place in the same Basilica as the event with Señora Laura and her Baby Jesus, but three years earlier.

November 8,[ii] 2011: Christy, Kandy, and I were in the Basilica at Montserrat, when the idea came to me to enter the confessional. Not to confess anything, but to cry with a captured audience.

And cry I did. I cried that my only child had died; I cried that I could not bear to live without him; and I cried that life was meaningless and I wanted to die. The Benedictine monk made no attempt to console me with the traditional platitudes, but sprang up, left the confessional, hugged me fiercely, and said with sure authority:

> "Oh, Señora! How very difficult. Your only child to die so quickly. So fast. Without warning. So difficult. But Jesus tells us that he is still here. Your son is still here and you still have a relationship with him. A VITAL relationship. Right now. Your son is not a fleck of dust. He is not just gone. He is *here*. You are to have a VITAL relationship with him here until you are called.

---

[i] On page xxviii of Richard Wilhelm's translation of the I-Ching, Carl Jung tells us that the original intent of *religio* (from *relegere*) is a careful observation and taking into account of the *numinous* (traditionally called spiritual) so that they can play their part in the life of the individual. In the theory of material realism, because the *numinous* is non-sensed, it is considered to be non-existent, or impossible to investigate. Thus, yet again, if one is to honor the *numinous*, right belief would *seem to be* the only option. More on this later.

[ii] Two years after this, I would be told to stay particularly alert on November 8, one of Uriel's feast days. Always document with dates.

Your work is to become aware of that relationship with your son and develop it – spirit to spirit. This is the message of Jesus."

"It is?" was all I could say. I had heard about Jesus all my life, but, most certainly, I had never heard this.

That night I was caught in horrific pain. Slipping in and out of sleep, I begged to see Aaron; I begged to be helped; I begged to die; and I begged to be able to understand the message of Jesus as understood by the monk. Then, a dream:

> I was with a group of teenagers. A boy walked by wearing a football jersey with the number 53 [Aaron's high school football number]. I fell to the ground. The kids asked, "What's wrong? What's wrong?" I stuttered, "My son died; my heart is broken. I want to die."

> I fainted, inside of the dream, and then AARON CAME. I could see his tattoo of Max. He hugged me. I felt his strong arms. He seemed to float. I said, "Aaron! Aaron! You are here!" He smiled wonderfully. Then I KNEW that I was in a dream and I knew to ask him, "Are you okay?"

> "Yes," he said. I insisted, "Are you REALLY okay? Can you come back?" Aaron laughed, "No, I can't come back. Anyway, I really DO like it here. But Mom ..." and then he got so serious. He told me to stop thinking about killing myself, that he was always with me, and to not be so sad.

December 28, 2011. Feeling absolutely compelled to do so, I called Aaron's dad Joe to tell him that 6 weeks ago, on his own father's birthday, a monk had told me that the message of Jesus is *to work to become aware of the presence of the dead in order to develop a vital relationship with them in spirit.* NOW, while we are alive.

I told Joe that I fell asleep begging to die to be with Aaron, and that Aaron came in a dream and told me not to be so sad, that he was always with me. And when I told him that Aaron had said, "I really do like it here, Mom," Joe began to cry.

Saying that he had not been able to find any comfort anywhere, Joe explained that he had gone to Christmas Mass to pray for only one thing: to know that Aaron was okay.

"Your calling me three days later, out of the blue, feels like the answer to my prayer," Joe told me. Our phone call ended with my *insisting* that Aaron was communicating by using the number 72.

Two days later, Joe was wondering with a friend in a restaurant. He wondered what or who had motivated me to call him with the message that Aaron "liked it where he was," three days after he had prayed to know that Aaron was okay.

He wondered about my insistence that Aaron was using the number 72 to communicate. "If that's true, why don't I get anything?" he asked his friend and then answered himself with, "I must be too stupid to see it."

While all this wondering was going on, Joe heard, very vaguely, a woman talking in the background and a little boy answering her. When the woman said, "Do you want to say hi to Daddy?" for some reason, Joe stood up in his booth and turned fully around to look at them. Joe wrote to me:

> There was a blonde-headed child like our boy at 3. He looked right at me and said, 'Hi, Daddy!' He had on a cap with **1972** printed on the visor. **CLICK. Joe felt his entire world shift.**

Joe confessed later that he had never really believed he was too stupid to be missing messages from the dead, but too smart to fall for such malarkey. Joe believed that he got no messages because there were no messages to be gotten. Period.

The fact that I had been "taken in by such nonsense" was Joe's proof-positive that grief can destroy even the most levelheaded of people.

My call "in answer to his Christmas prayer," opened Joe's mind to wonder and he stumbled over the mysterious truth that little boys can deliver big messages: numbers can be used *symbolically* by the dead to make their presence known.

If you choose to soak your beliefs in the healing balm of wonder, you might also choose to begin to investigate *the possibility* that communication from the dead is embedded in our everyday walk-about world, just waiting to be claimed by the discerning mind.

If so, you might choose to begin your investigation by *claiming numbers as symbols*.

Directive 5: Claim Numbers as Symbols

"In the sorrow of separation from their loved ones, fools cry for awhile and then forget, but the wise find the impulse to seek their lost love in the heart of the eternal."

–Paramahansa Yogananda

Humanity becomes aware of the sacred *because it shows itself to us.* And it does so by using ordinary objects *symbolically.*[9]

As I struggled to understand what these words could be pointing to, I learned that the only ordinary thing about numbers was my way of thinking about them.

I toiled to get a glimmer of meaning when I read that the Pythagoreans considered numbers to be divine and that they taught that the universe could be best understood in terms of whole numbers.

My mind protested when I read, "numbers are autonomous entities with lives of their own, *pre-existent to matter*, [my italics] and a link to the Cosmos."[10]

And I all but gave up when I read that models of the invisible realm, in which this material realm is embedded, could best be understood as made up of forms, "meaning mathematical forms or numerical patterns: not patterns of energy or matter, but just plain *numbers.*"[11]

I don't understand what any of this is saying, but I do know what is meant, for I have had the *experience* of numbers behaving like autonomous entities, signaling unperceived doors into sacred dimensions. Quite often in fact.

And I could feel that Aaron and others said to be dead were involved in the compellingly persuasive events that led to the claiming of numbers as symbols, but I could not figure out *how spirit could possibly manipulate matter.*

My "need to understand how spirit could manipulate matter" was nothing more than my defending another unconsciously absorbed underlying assumption of material realism: *causality*.

As matter is all there is, goes the theory, everything (including thoughts, feelings, ideas, and beliefs) is *caused* by matter acting upon matter. If a *material cause* for an event cannot be detected, the event is a glitch.[i]

It was assumed by materialists (followers of material realism) that glitches are simply "results whose causes have not yet been found."

Traditionally, glitches have been dismissed by slapping on labels such as "curious coincidences," or "miracles."

Carl Jung[ii] broke the Western tradition of dismissing glitches by hypothesizing that events may be *caused* or connected by something other than matter interacting with matter. The term he coined for his *a-causal* mechanism is *synchronicity* and he proposed *meaning* as the mechanism of connection/cause.

Because we have absorbed material realism's underlying assumption of *causality,* synchronicity throws us for quite a loop, but:

> Synchronicity is no more baffling or mysterious than the discontinuities of physics. It is only the *ingrained belief in the sovereign power of causality* [my italics] that creates intellectual difficulties and makes it appear unthinkable that causeless events exist or could ever exist.[12]

---

[i] A glitch is always, and only, a glitch in a *theory*. There are no glitches in reality, only glitches in our understanding.

[ii] Carl Jung's work profoundly influences religious studies, literature, philosophy, archaeology, mythology, psychiatry, psychology, history, anthropology, alchemy, physics, astrology, astronomy, mathematics, and more.

It was gratifying to read Jung's assertion that, "synchronicity and numbers were always brought into connection with one another," as it supported my feeling that there is *meaning* in the claimed numbers that kept appearing synchronistically.

Aniceto's Number: On January 22, 2002, my father-in-law Aniceto was sitting in his rocking chair as I tied his shoelaces. He exhaled a huge breath of this life on me and I knew it was his last. I ventured to say, "Alejo, your dad is dying. Let's just try to get him back to bed and help him go."

Instantly, I denied what was so clearly visible, as the fearful often do. In a terrible panic, Aaron and Alejo carried Aniceto, in his rocking chair, to the car. Alejo drove frantically to the hospital. Aaron sat in the backseat, his eyes full of tears of confusion. I chanted to Aniceto that everything was going to be fine. We kept ourselves firmly in denial all the way to the hospital… .

As Alejo wandered the wild, unknown (to him) side of Life that we call death, seeking his father, it soon became very clear that death was no sort of dead end at all. As meaningful patterns and hidden resonances emerged out of the mist, I did my part without knowing what I was doing. I documented.

The year that his father died, Alejo was working in their home country of Spain. On May 28 of 2002, Alejo was having a particularly bad day. Overwhelmed by guilt, grief, and regret, he kept providing me with proof after proof of how he had done everything wrong.

He had not brought his dad back to Spain; he had been too impatient, too grumpy, too horribly this and too terribly that. Alejo was, he insisted, a hopelessly inadequate son. Suddenly, we both became aware of the number 22 popping up in curiously repetitive ways.

This was important. Aniceto had claimed 2 as "his number" sixty years prior to his death on January 22, 2002.

Alejo and I left hotel room 122 to have coffee at a sidewalk cafe. We watched a car with license plate 122 pull out, and we watched another with plate 222 pull in. I sat on the steps of a house to watch a parade, not realizing (until we saw the photo) that it was house No. 22. Lunch cost 22.00 euro, and we sat at table number 22 for dinner. 22 was *everywhere*. All weekend.

Driving home, Alejo wondered, "Could all those 22s really be connected to my dad? Maybe if we choose any number and pay attention to it ..." At that moment, a truck passed and on the back panel we read, "For moving service, call 222-2222."

Selective Perception: It is important to take a moment to examine our (Alejo's and mine) unconscious defense of causality. Our first reaction to the synchronistic appearances of 22 was to call them a result of "selective perception."

Selective perception is a term used to describe the human behavior of scanning our surroundings for things that we are interested in, while ignoring the rest. Marketing relies extensively on selective perception, and uses great care and precision to create signs and logos to link specific products to the particular interests of consumers.

If selective perception can account for our becoming aware of the 22s, it would mean that the 22s existed in what we call objective reality and we were simply honing in on what existed – because we were particularly interested in it.

This is very different from the synchronistic appearance of *symbols*. A sign, once it is invented, *exists*. But a *symbol* is more like a birthing – a birthing of the sacred something that is showing itself to us *into the realm of matter*. And we participate in the birth:

Synchronicity takes the coincidence of events in space and time as meaning something more than mere chance, namely, a peculiar interdependence of objective events among themselves as well as with the subjective (psychic) states of the observer or observers.[13]

Jung's theory of synchronicity with its "peculiar interdependence of objective events with the subjective (psychic) states of the observers,"[i] *allows for the possibility* that the consciousness of those we call living can collaborate with the consciousness of those we call dead to "birth events" in the realm of matter.

On page 194 of his book, *Jung: The Mystic*, Gary Lachman says:

Jung hints at but never declares outright: that synchronicities are, as Colin Wilson suggests, 'a kind of nudge from some unknown guardian angel, whose purpose is to tell us that life is not as meaningless as it looks,' a form of the "spirit hypothesis."

For over 5000 years theologians, philosophers, theoretical scientists, and respected scholars have been postulating an essential reality in an invisible space acting on this one. Yet ...

To many scientists such thoughts are upsetting. The view is widespread that science shouldn't get involved with such issues. It should be useful and technical, but not inspiring; logical but mindless. However, we should have the courage for an enlightened and liberated science that does more than serve stockholder equity. We must make an effort to understand the nature of reality: the empirical and nonempirical, the material and the spiritual.[14]

---

[i] *Objective events* are experiences that fire the body's physical senses of sight, hearing, smell, taste, and touch. *Subjective events* are experiences that do not. *Psychic*: related to the soul or mind. Events are said to be psychic when they cannot be explained by "natural law" which is nothing more than another way of saying cannot be explained by material realism.

Back to Aniceto and his 22: Two days after "the weekend of the 22s," I was in line at a Spanish social security office, waiting to get information. A woman cut in front of me but, because I insisted on my place, I got to the number dispenser in the right order to pull number **222**. Alejo and I **claimed 22** as Aniceto's symbol for communication.

Eight years later: On October 21, 2010, Aaron's friend Tom was showing me the "football bus" that Aaron had told me so much about. Suddenly, everything was more than I could bear. I ran to Aaron's car for comfort, turned the key, and saw **2:22** on the digital clock. I thought of Aniceto.

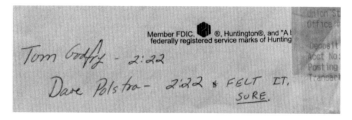

The next day I had a meeting with Aaron's lawyer. I arrived to find the office door unlocked, but the office itself empty. I reclined on a sofa and promptly fell asleep. Jolting awake, I checked the time: **2:22. Aniceto! Click. I FELT IT SURE.**

Four years later I was working on this section of the book, totally dismayed at my inability to convey the tremendous *knowing* that had come with Aniceto's **2:22** in Indiana. I complained aloud, "Aniceto, this is too big. You started the whole thing. Alejo's your kid; convince him to help us." *Exactly then* my dear friend Karen sent the message shown above.

> Cathy! I woke up out of a dead sleep and looked at the clock. It was 2:22. I had a very strong feeling this meant something. Those numbers don't have meaning to me personally but I know there can be communication through numbers from those trying to help us.
> 10:31 AM
>
> So, I will try to learn of those numbers have a specific meaning. 10:31 AM
>
> Oh my god Karen. It is my father un law. I am of course working on the book. I am going to send an email to you with some information
> Oh my god... 10:32 AM

Because Karen knew that there could be communication through numbers from "those trying to help us," (meaning the dead) she honored her very strong feeling that 2:22 meant something.

Thanks to her collaboration, we learned that Aaron's instructions "to put people in contact with each other," can be done by claimed numbers reaching someone *who will relay the message.*

Richard's number: When my dad Richard entered hospice "to rest for a bit," I told him that Alejo's dad had communicated with us by using numbers – after his death.

Dad immediately chose 5-2-2-8 as his number and we agreed that the four numbers could be in any order because "four numbers are hard to get." It should not have been surprising, but it was, when nine days later, dear Richard Jensen left his body behind.

For forty-nine days, I lit a candle three times a day and read to my dad from *The Tibetan Book of the Dead*, changing the Buddhist imagery to Christian imagery more familiar to us. It was very comforting.

This book states that approximately seventeen days after death a person can begin to send messages, and advises the reader to be alert. Nineteen days after Dad's walk into death, I was getting ready for my own morning walk when Alejo said, "I have bad news for you. I am going to walk with you today."

That really surprised me, as Alejo almost never just "goes for a walk with me," morning or otherwise. Not then. Not now.

Alejo wandered off here and there, and after a while, he came and asked me, "Which daughter are you for your dad?" (There are six.) Raising my arms, I declared, **"Baby Girl No. 2!"**

Motioning me to follow him, we left the beaten path, pushed through some bushes, and climbed under a barbed wire fence to arrive at an old rickety boat dock completely hidden from view. There he showed me a boat with Dad's four numbers and **Baby Girl 2**.

No one is saying that my dad magically put that boat there – just that these things make you wonder. Or, at least they *could*:

Why did Alejo "decide" to walk with me? Why did he "decide" to crawl through bushes and under a rusty old barbed wire fence? And why in the world did he ask me, "Which daughter are you for your dad?" He very well knew that Christy is the only older sister that I have – he had enjoyed her company for close to thirty years.

And where did the *exact words*, **"Baby Girl 2,"** which I heard myself say, come from?

Dad changes his number: On January 19, 2010, I dreamed:

> I heard Dad's voice calling out and I said, "He sounds good, just tired." I saw a quarter moon carved on a bedroom door. It was signed *Cathy 1979*. I didn't remember having carved it and I kept figuring out my age. 55 [the year I was born], 65, 75. Wow, I was **23**. That is too old to be carving on their door. I figured it out repeatedly, "55-65-75, I was **23**. **23**. **23**." [My dad's wife] Linda said, "When you made that, you came upstairs and told us that now you knew what a quarter moon looked like."

Three days after my dream, I got an e-mail from Linda:

Cathy, I had a strange dream the other night.[i] I saw a big dot, like a ball, then a line ending with another ball and I saw my hand, or I think it was my hand, drawing the number **23**."

CLICK. Something big was happening. And it was happening with Dad. There is nothing so spectacular about Linda's "connecting the dots" dream to qualify it as the *only dream in fifty years that she has felt the need to share with me* – three days after my own 23 dream, and on the anniversary of Aniceto's death.

The **23** simmered as I visited Aaron and Kandy. I barely blinked and that whole world vanished. But the 23 lie waiting.

November 2012: Practicing a lucid dreaming technique,[ii] I fell asleep "asking for clarification of the 23." Waking up, I saw Aaron's number **72** and the number **23** flashing together on a marquee-like thing.

That afternoon, as Alejo and I were walking home from a store, I began to wonder aloud about the 23 dreams and the morning experience of the flashing 72 and 23. Suddenly I couldn't think straight. I was disoriented. I stopped, paralyzed in confusion.

Alejo tapped my shoulder gently. "Turn around," he said. The entire store window was full of Rams **23**. We **claimed 23** as Dad's new number.

---

[i] Perhaps we had the dream on the same night. Document with dates.
[ii] Research on lucid dreaming, visitation dreams, and consciously dreaming with the dead (and much more) is extensive, and easy to find.

Aaron's Number 72: When Aaron died on 7–2 (July 2), the only attractive thing about death not being a dead end was the possibility that I could die and be with him now.

That pain had me plotting and scheming ways out of "here" that could pass for an accident. Wave after wave would take me, would bowl me over, would have me falling and swooning, my legs collapsing in the most inappropriate and most public of places.

That pain had me crumpled me into small wounded mounds in airport corners and on train depot benches, had me clutching strangers in churches, supermarkets, rest stops, and patios. The only thing I could do, I did. I documented.

Aaron was born in 1972 and he left on 7–2, 2010. He used 72 in passwords and addresses on the web. 72 seemed his logical number and I was ever alert. What follows are a few of the initial 72s that encouraged me as I limped along.

Cabs with 72: The cab that took us to Aaron's service in Barcelona had registration number **2772**. The one that brought us back had registration number **2727** and plate **3672**.

Claiming 72: Christy came to Barcelona. The day after Aaron's funeral, we walked to the chapel where, only 3 months earlier, I had gone to Easter Mass with Aaron and his friends. Suddenly, *that pain* took me into a daydream/vision of Aaron picking me up and carrying me across a bridge. At that moment, a man who very much resembled Aaron walked by, wearing a T-shirt with only the number **72** on it. Christy and I **claimed 72** as Aaron's number.

Kandy claims 27: The airplane taking Kandy back to Spain (after Aaron's service in Iowa) had screens on the back of every seat. Suddenly, all the screens that she could see went blank and for a few seconds **0207** appeared on every one.

This is "el dos de julio" (the second of July) in Spanish. It is, of course, the mirror image of 72 as well. **Kandy claimed 27 as Aaron's number.**

Campground 72: On my way to Indiana to take care of Aaron's things, I slept in a campground. When the ranger gave me receipt **1577772,** I asked him if it was because I had chosen campsite #72.  "No. It's just random," he said as he handed me the next receipt, as proof.

Page 772 and Sister Luke: As mentioned earlier, the important words, *"I will speak of your decrees before nobles without being ashamed,"* came on page **772.**

Bank account: I closed Aaron's bank account and opened a new one to receive some money owed to him. The poor bank manager, so young and eager to help, did not know what to do with a woman weeping so deeply over a "randomly generated account number," that other women joined in. I tried to comfort a woman who kept crying, "Oh no! Not Aaron!" by explaining about the number 72 and showing her the new account number ending in **72.**

The debit card with 72's: When the debit card came full of 72s, I called the bank to verify that the 72s were not because the account ended in 72. "No, it's random," I was told. I knew it was not, and I worked diligently to not dismiss everything as "curious coincidences."

Another little boy with a big 72 message: Because Alejo heeded his mother's request to pay her water bill *now*, he participated in a powerful event. His report:

> On the way to town, I saw 72s everywhere, one after the other. I got to the water company and waited in line to pay the bill. A little boy, about four or so, tried to play peek-a-boo with me, but I didn't want to get involved, and I ignored him.
>
> The little boy played around calmly until he and his mom were about to enter the office. Suddenly, he burst into tears and started screaming, "The message is on the T-shirt! The message is on the T-shirt!"
>
> Everyone got very nervous. The mother scolded the little boy to be quiet, but she made no impact. He just continued to repeat, in a desperate sort of way, "The message is on the T-shirt! The message is on the T-shirt!" Everyone became silent as the little boy continued to cry and repeat the same words, over, and over.
>
> Suddenly I thought, "What message is on the T-shirt?" and I walked over to look at his shirt: *Penn Basketball 1972.*

***A Course in Miracles* and page 272:** When *A Course in Miracles* arrived, I closed my eyes, breathed deeply, and prayed for a message.

Ever so slowly, I fingered the 1400 pages of my new book, and opened to page **272**.

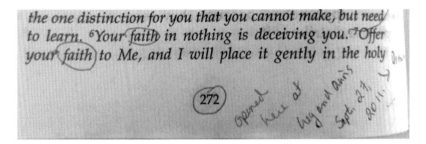

Aaron and his grandpa Richard: Claiming Dad's new number as 23 goes as reported, but the rest of the story was saved until Aaron's number had been formally introduced.

When my camera fused shut with battery acid and grief, I didn't care – so sure was I that I would *never* take another picture in what was left of my life. My sister-in-law Ann's gentle words as she handed me a new camera touched me deeply, "It's to take pictures of the miracles, Cathy."

I decided I would use my new camera for the first time, and for its intended purpose. I returned to the store the next morning to take a picture of Dad's 23. One poster had been added to the window display: RAMS. TWENTY-THREE. **EST. 1972.**

My number 55: Born in 1955, I have long claimed 55 as my personal number. I wrote my niece Laura on my 55th birthday, "I feel like I am going to learn a lot this year. I hope I'm not going to die." Of course *that* Cathy did die, **5** months and **5** days later.

This is the jersey that Aaron was wearing when he left behind the body that needed it. The paramedics cut it in half, trying to do something.

But there was nothing to be done on that one and only July 2 (7-2) in this lifetime, when I was 55 years, 5 months and (5 hours short of) 5 days.

Aaron, Aniceto, and Cathy: In our last picture together, Aaron is wearing Aniceto's 22.

Wearing his shirt, I passed a mirror …

2018 – just to show that the messaging does not stop: I knew, for months, that I needed to cancel my Amazon Prime account. It did not work in Spain, and I was wasting money.

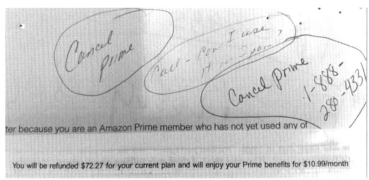

ter because you are an Amazon Prime member who has not yet used any of

You will be refunded $72.27 for your current plan and will enjoy your Prime benefits for $10.99/month

But, I just didn't get around to it, until the other day when, for some reason, I finally did. I was refunded **$72.27**.

To claim a number as a *symbol* is to recognize that *something sacred is showing itself to you*, and to acknowledge that "that something" is, somehow, connected to your dead.

To compile a database of claimed numbers is to investigate that connection. This will not be done by anyone who:

- *believes* that investigating a connection with the dead is forbidden and/or dangerous.

- *believes* that opening-door events are miracles and feels that investigating miracles diminishes their value.

- *believes* that death cannot be investigated without dying.

- *believes* that material realism is fact rather than theory, and, consequently, dismisses these experiences as coincidental.

- *believes* that life is a meaningless trip from a maternity ward to a crematorium and, consequently, is not motivated to research any further.

How can one break through such barriers of beliefs? Viktor Frankl[i] provides a key in his book *Man's Search for Meaning:*

> What is demanded of man is not, as some existential philosophers teach, to endure the meaninglessness of life, but rather to bear his incapacity to grasp its unconditional meaningfulness in rational terms.[15]

A man who lost everything in horrifyingly meaningless conditions tells us that life is *unconditionally meaningful,* but we don't get it. We don't get it, he says, because we lack the capacity to *grasp the fact rationally.*

Frankl does not advocate accepting our incapacity and maintaining a positive attitude in the midst of horror. Instead, he demonstrates that attempting to comprehend the sacred something that *shows itself to us* develops the capacity to grasp life's unconditional meaningfulness in rational terms.

"Attempting to comprehend the sacred" has traditionally been called *seeking,* and it has long been stated that whoever seeks shall find. *But you have to seek beyond your beliefs.*

Believers in material realism won't do that. Neither will believers in the creed that "God prefers belief to knowledge."

This refusal to seek beyond belief, however, says nothing about the sacred something that shows itself to us. It speaks only to the human tendency to defend beliefs and cling to outdated, inadequate models. It's time for seekers to model-up.

---

[i] Austrian neurologist and psychiatrist Viktor Frankl had chosen "suicide prevention" as his Great and Holy Work long before he was deported to Auschwitz concentration camp in 1944. Frankl hypothesized that human nature is motivated by the search for a life purpose, and he founded *logotherapy* as a method to find it.

Directive 6: Model-Up

"The only *thing that is unqualifiedly good is extended vision, the enlargement of one's understanding of the nature of things."*
                                                                        –Huston Smith

The need to model-up is glaringly obvious, but only when looking to the past: the earth has never been flat, nor was it ever the center of the universe; beating the devil out of sick patients did not make for a successful cure nor did lobotomies make good citizens, in spite of sure belief that these things were so.

It is as easy to chuckle at the beliefs of the "naive peoples of the past" as it is to be shocked at how vigorously they defended those beliefs. It is not so easy, however, to chuckle over the fact that the beliefs we defend today and the methods we use to defend them, will also be seen as shockingly naive, someday.

The important point is not the absurdity or the accuracy of the specific beliefs, but the act of defending belief rather than enlarging our understanding of the nature of things.

Defending belief is such common behavior that Max Planck, the founder of quantum physics, put what I call "modeling-up" into a simple maxim, as apt for religion as it is for science:

> A new scientific truth does normally not prevail in the way that its opponents become convinced and declare that they have learned something, but rather because its opponents eventually die out, and the following generation is familiar with the truth from the outset.

Belief that the Bible was a literal account of God's creation defined the West for centuries. This vision of sacred scripture was so widespread and unquestioned that defense strategies were not really needed until the 16th century.

As Copernicus, Galileo, and other ardent believers in God extended their vision *beyond the literal interpretation* of the Bible, the more ferociously was that belief defended.

By the turn of the 17th century, the belief that the Biblical account of creation was literal fact ruled the West with an iron fist. Constructive doubt[i] had become very risky, and publishing theories that challenged the belief in the Bible as geology[ii] had become extremely dangerous. All innovation was coming to a standstill.

A solution materialized around the time of Giordano Bruno's[iii] execution, and Rene Descartes is credited for having come up with the idea.

In 1597, nineteen-year-old Descartes was camped with a French army near Ulm, Germany, when what he calls an angel of truth told him that *the conquest of nature is to be achieved through number and measurement.*

Not surprisingly, Descartes took this as his mission and created methods of number and measurement more than adequate to accomplish his angel-given task.[iv]

---

[i] *Constructive doubt:* an intelligent questioning. *Destructive doubt:* a mental habit of skepticism, which prevents the seeking of truth.

[ii] Archbishop James Ussher meticulously calculated Biblical dates to ascertain that creation had taken place about 6 p.m. on October 22, 4004 BCE. This belief resulted in fossils being thrown away as "strange rock formations" until a mere two and a half centuries ago.

[iii] *Giordano Bruno:* Italian philosopher, astronomer, and mathematician burned at the stake in the year 1600 for refusing to withdraw his hypothesis that stars are suns with living planetary systems of their own, fostering life throughout the universe.

[iv] Called the Father of the Modern Scientific Method and the Father of Philosophy as well, Descartes' contributions to the quest of extending vision and enlarging understanding are vast. In the field of number and measurement alone, he uncovered analytical geometry – used in the discovery of infinitesimal calculus and analysis, and much more.

Assuming that the nature to be conquered by number and measurement was the world of matter, the non-countable, unmeasurable world of spirit was left in the hands of those thought to know it best: the Church.

By preserving a distinct arena for the church, while limiting its interference in scientific investigation, exploration of *material reality* could continue.

At the time of Descartes' angelic visit, Mechanical Philosophy was the popular model/metaphor for the nature of reality. This theory assumed that *everything* was reducible to mechanical laws, and it held scientists responsible for uncovering the clocklike mechanisms making the visible universe tick.

Isaac Newton was certainly up to the task, but there was a problem. Many of his observations contradicted the "universe as a machine" metaphor. Not easily defeated by theory, Newton began scrutinizing the alchemic metaphor for the nature of reality, which, because it did not assume that matter was the ground of all being, was expansive enough to accommodate his data.

And so it was that some two decades later, Newton tamed a mysteriously non-sensed, but very real force. An apple bonking him on the head gets all the glory, as crediting invisible voices encoded in alchemy has been consistently ignored or embarrassingly denied. Until recently.

Newton's model/metaphor is called Classical Physics,[i] and it has been extremely successful in conquering the world of nature by number and measurement. With time, its Cartesian component of separating nature into the two investigative

---

[i] Newtonian Classical Physics, Scientific Materialism, Material Realism and Physicalism are some of the other names given to models sharing the same basic assumption that everything, including consciousness, comes from matter.

camps of science and religion, morphed from a 17th century compromise into an 18th century belief that "matter" and "spirit" *really are* two separate worlds. Most of us have inherited this belief. And most of us defend it.

Just the other day in fact, while discussing opening-door events, I was handed a piece of paper with the words *Spirit* and *Matter* written in different colors. Two-directional arrows pointed back and forth and "NO INTERSECTION" and "EXCLUSIVE" were capitalized. For emphasis.

I was not impressed, however, having had too much *experience* that contradicts the model, and I reminded the Cartesian enthusiast that the *belief* in two mutually exclusive worlds labeled matter **or** spirit began with a boy in a body of matter receiving a message from a spirit/angel. A non-exclusivity of the two worlds if ever there was one.

Newton's new model was so successful at explaining and conquering the world of nature that the belief in "two mutually exclusive realms of Spirit and Matter" narrowed down into a belief in only *one* world. The world of matter.

These are the materialists and material realism is their *metaphor* for the nature of reality. But most of them (us) believe it to be a fact.

Scientists who (unconsciously) believe that material realism is a fact are not true scientists. They are "pseudo-scientists" *unable* to practice essential science. They use the name of science, but their *beliefs* hobble their ability to theorize, and structure their every experiment.[i]

---

[i]Poking a brain here while measuring an increase of blood flow there, does not prove that the brain *produces* consciousness. Not matter how often it is done. Poking here, while measuring there, could just as easily prove that poking around in the brain interferes with the *processing* of consciousness.

The same thing happens in the field of investigation known as religion, when its vital role as an open-ended, error-correcting growth system is co-opted by the "pseudo-religious," whose only goal is to defend inherited beliefs about The Bible.

Pseudo-religion has so absorbed material realism's basic tenet that matter is all that there is, that it insists (quite ruthlessly at times) that the symbols and metaphors provided by our spiritual heroes are referencing *the world of matter*.

But symbols *never* reference the material world and metaphors are *never* facts. Joseph Campbell explains:

> God is a metaphor for a mystery that absolutely transcends all human categories of thought, even the categories of being and non-being. Those are categories of thought. I mean it's as simple as that. So it depends on how much you want to think about it. Whether it is putting you in touch with the mystery that's the ground of your own being. If it isn't, well, it's a lie.

> So half the people in the world are religious people who think that their metaphors are facts. Those are what we call theists. The other half are people who know that the metaphors are not facts. And so, they're lies. Those are the atheists.[16]

Western Culture is so permeated with pseudo-science and pseudo-religion's (unconscious) belief that "the *theory* of material realism is a fact" that most of us are convinced that there is no way to *know* anything at all about death without dying – if even then. This is in stark contrast to what we have been told for millennia: **Seek** and you shall find.

In about 1850 or so, seekers in a new religion called Spiritualism issued the first world-wide challenge to material realism's claim that matter (brain) *produces* consciousness.

Spiritualist reports detailing experiences with apparitions, clairvoyant visions, precognitive dreams, and influential mediums contacting the dead, spread like wild fire. Soon, people began their own experimenting. With duplicated results. Worldwide.

The funny thing about Spiritualism is that many of the people participating were highly educated. And not only that – internationally known, well-respected and extremely rational scientists[i] were actively researching Spiritualists claims and publishing their findings Or, at least they were trying to.

By 1850, burning heretics at the stake had been abandoned, but clinging to outdated models had continued almost unabated. Many of the first scientists to investigate Spiritualist claims were blacklisted; their careers destroyed; their families, uprooted; and their children, traumatized.

Their response was to found institutions where research into *aspects of consciousness as yet unknown to science* could be published for worldwide debate. One such institute is the Society for Psychical Research (SPR). Its intent:

> To approach these varied problems without prejudice or prepossession of any kind, and in the same spirit of exact and unimpassioned enquiry which has enabled science to solve so many problems, once not less obscure nor less hotly debated.[17]

Least you imagine SPR members as sincere but naive ghost hunters holding hands in haunted houses, look up the

---

[i] Says Arthur Conan Doyle in his book, *The New Revelation*: When I regarded Spiritualism as a vulgar delusion of the uneducated, I could afford to look down upon it; but when it was endorsed by men like Crookes, whom I knew to be the most rising British chemist, by Wallace, who was the rival of Darwin and by Flammarion, the best known of astronomers, I could not afford to dismiss it. It was all very well to throw down the books of these men which contained their mature conclusions and careful investigations, and to say 'Well, he has one weak spot in his brain' *but a man has to be very self-satisfied if the day does not come when he wonders if the weak spot is not in his own brain* [my italics].

membership logs or at least the rosters of past presidents. There you will find Nobel Prizes, decorated discoveries, coveted recognitions, and prestigious awards sprinkled on SPR members like salt on popcorn.

The challenge to material realism continues, as true spiritual researchers[i] and essential scientists carry on the human quest for meaning. Which includes the quest to understand *what death means.* Their proposals may surprise you.

Whether we the common folk know it or not, the scientific model of the nature of reality called material realism was modeled-up more than one hundred years ago.

The *current* model rejects the notion that matter is the ground of all being, separate and exclusive from a (possibly existing) "spirit world." The *current* model, in fact, hypothesizes that both worlds are real. ***And that both worlds are one.***

On page 2 of Amit Goswami's book, *The Self-Aware Universe: How Consciousness Creates the Material World,* we read:

> During the past four hundred years, we have gradually adopted the belief that science can be built *only* on the notion that everything is made of matter – of so-called atoms in the void. We have come to accept materialism dogmatically, despite its failure to account for the most familiar experiences of our daily lives. In short, we have an inconsistent worldview.

---

[i] Einstein has been quoted as saying, "A contemporary has said, not unjustly, that in this materialistic age of ours the serious scientific workers are the only profoundly religious people." Contributions from authentically religious scientists fill page after page of the documented human quest for understanding. A *very* small sampling of recent contributors: Monsignor Georges Lemaitre, Pierre Teilhard de Chardin, SJ, Rabbi Aryeh Kaplan, and Seyyid Hossein Nasr.

Our predicament has fueled the demand for a new paradigm – a unifying worldview that will integrate mind and spirit into science...The centerpiece of this new paradigm is the recognition that modern science validates an ancient idea – the idea that consciousness, not matter, is the ground of all being.

The *current* Post-Newtonian paradigm/model of the nature of reality hypothesizes that consciousness *is* before matter *manifests*. Its underlying assumptions look something like this:

And as a man who has devoted his whole life to the most clearheaded science, to the study of matter, I can tell you as a result of my research about the atoms this much: There is no matter as such! All matter originates and exists only by virtue of a force which brings the particle of an atom to vibration and holds this most minute solar system of the atom together. We must assume behind this force the existence of a conscious and intelligent mind. This mind is the matrix of all matter. I regard consciousness as fundamental. I regard matter as derivative from consciousness. We cannot get behind consciousness (Max Planck, born 1858).

Any transformation in the material aspect of the Earth is a manifestation of spiritual forces lying behind matter. But if we go further and further back in time we eventually arrive at a point in evolution where matter first began to exist. This material element developed out of the spiritual. Before this point, only the spiritual element was present (Rudolf Steiner, born 1861).

There is neither spirit nor matter in the world; the stuff of the universe is *spirit-matter*. No other substance but this could produce the human molecule. I remain convinced that the objections made to it arise from the mere fact that few people can make up their minds to abandon an old point of view and take the risk of a new idea (Teilhard de Chardin, born 1881).

Everything we call real is made of things that cannot be regarded as real (Niels Bohr, born 1885).

Consciousness is absolutely fundamental. It cannot be accounted for in terms of anything else (Erwin Schrodinger, born 1887).

In the field of consciousness research – and also in physics and astronomy – we are breaking past the cause-and-effect, mechanistic way of interpreting things. In the biological sciences, there is a vitalism coming in that goes much further toward positing a common universal consciousness of which our brain is simply an organ (Joseph Campbell, born 1904).

The constituents of real things are found not to be real – these findings show that the quantum phenomena make it possible to establish a new covenant between the human mind and the mind-like background of the universe (Lothar Schafer, born 1939).

Unconscious materialists unconsciously defend their belief that without a brain made of matter there is no consciousness, i.e., there is no life. Their defense mechanisms include a refusal to investigate the possibility of collaboration with the dead, and/or a vague uneasiness about promoting it.

I had a touch of that vague uneasiness myself, and it was due to my fear that those who kept insisting, "The Bible forbids collaboration with the dead" might be right. But they are not right. But, then again, they are not exactly wrong either. It all depends on how you define the words *forbid* and *dead.*

If you are (unconsciously) a materialist and restrict the word *dead* to its meaning of "people whose physical bodies no longer function," and if you restrict *forbid* to its meaning of "not allow," you will believe that the Bible warns against collaboration with the physically dead.

Consider though, that *forbid* also means *to create conditions of impossibility* as in "the narrow street forbids a U-turn," or more to the point here: belief in material realism *forbids* collaboration with the *dead* because it (the belief) creates conditions of impossibility.

Those unwilling to consider what lies beyond their belief that "Biblical dead" is talking about physical bodies *are* the dead.

Their self-imposed inability to experience their own immortality *forbids* (creates conditions of impossibility) any collaboration with them; it is a waste of time to try. Better to let the dead bury the dead and work with the *living* – those who seek truth beyond their beliefs.

The status of the physical bodies of those we call *dead* and the status of the physical bodies of those we call *living* is immaterial, as none of this is about physical bodies.[i]

The only thing forbidding collaboration with the dead is your closed door of belief. It is your door. You are the one who made it and you are the one who keeps it closed. And you are the only one who can open it.

When you do, *your* belief that the brain produces consciousness and *your* assumption that God prefers belief to knowledge, will melt like the Wicked Witch of the West in the Land of Oz, and *your* research into how the scarecrow knew what he knew, without having a brain, can begin.

---

[i] The (unconscious) belief in material realism's assumption that matter is what really matters explains the obsession with the *physical body*. It must be woken or resurrected because, without it, there is no Life. The trumpet call that, in the twinkling of an eye, resurrects or awakens the *dead* is the same trumpet call that, when heeded, leads to the learning of a mode of experiencing the supernormal realm of human spiritual life where the dead live and immortality is *experienced. Right now*.

Directive 7: Study, Search, and Research

"If we knew what it was we were doing,
it would not be called research, would it?"

–*Albert Einstein*

Inherited beliefs fill our heads and break our hearts:

- This is a mechanical universe brought into being by the inherent properties of matter.

- Consciousness is the by-product of the random movements of matter.

- The brain secretes thoughts and feelings, just as the liver secretes bile.

- There is no individual life beyond the grave.

Additionally, and in spite of the fact that, seeking truth is the catalyst for the *experience* on which all religions are founded, various (pseudo) religious traditions continue to bequeath the belief that "faith without inquiry" is more pleasing to God than is investigation.

Many cling to these beliefs as a man without a lifeboat clings to a sinking ship. For this reason, and this reason only, common experiences are labeled para-this and supernormal-that by pseudo-science and pseudo-religion.

They are "para/supernormal" only to the narrow parameters of unexamined beliefs, be they scientific or religious.

As you begin your research, keep in mind more advice from Einstein, particularly apt for today's lay researchers: "The only thing that you absolutely have to know is the location of the library."

That is, do not rely on the internet, wonderful though it is. Case in point: Sir Oliver Lodge.

Oliver Lodge joined the aforementioned Society for Psychical Research (SPR) soon after its founding. He was an active member while finishing his doctorate, while transmitting the world's first radio signal a year before Marconi, and while being decorated five times for his innovative work in thermal-conductivity and electricity. He was the acting president of the SPR when knighted for his numerous scientific contributions.

Knowing this, imagine my surprise to "learn" on the Web that Lodge's interest in the survival of consciousness was a result of his grief over the death of his son Raymond.

It is unquestionably a fact that Lodge was grieving his loved and vanished child. It is also unquestionably a fact that for 33 years *before* Raymond died, Lodge had been researching consciousness and publishing extensively on the implications of his findings: *consciousness is not dependent upon a body.* Watch out for pathologies of knowing and learning. Particularly your own.

Telepathy

When F. W. H. Myers[i] coined the term *telepathy* in 1882, global discussion of "transmitting information mind to mind" (long documented by professionals[ii] and amateurs[iii] alike) was greatly facilitated.

Design and conduct your own experiments and you may be led (as many others have been) to notice a dislocation between mind and body. This may lead you (as it has led many others) to research the possibility of survival of consciousness.

---

[i] Fredric Myers developed one of the first (if not the first) comprehensive theories of the unconscious mind.

[ii] A very small sampling: The Institute of Noetic Sciences, Starlab, and the U.S. government. Dean Radin, Rupert Sheldrake, and Julie Beischel.

[iii] A very small sampling: Mark Twain, Upton Sinclair, and Jack London.

Telepathy experiment: On Aaron's birthday, four of us designed a telepathy experiment:

1. Each person writes the name of an animal on a small piece of paper, which is kept out of sight.
2. Set a timer for seven minutes.
3. The sender focuses on her animal, trying to keep only the image of the animal in mind for the seven minutes.
4. When the timer buzzes, the receivers count together: 1, 2, … and on 3, they *simultaneously* shout out the name of the animal that had come to their minds.

We began. Three tries resulted in nothing of note, but on the fourth and last try: The sender sent the image and the receivers did their best to receive it. The timer rang and we all counted 1, 2, and on 3, we simultaneously shouted, as if of one mind, "BIRD." The animal was a bat.

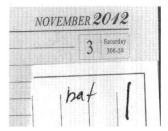

Sending images: Alejo and I practiced "sending images to each other and to Aaron" as we were falling asleep.[i]

Alejo: It's weird really to get these images in your head.
Cathy: Yes, it is. I see some women and girls wearing old-fashioned bonnets.
Alejo: Yes. Hmm. Me, too. Where are they?
Cathy: In some old town in the United States. There are wooden sidewalks. There's a dog.
Alejo: What kind of a dog?
Cathy: An old yellow dog.
Alejo: Hmm. Me, too.
Cathy: Remember to send the symbol for Aaron to get to me.

---

[i] Alejo and I were unknowingly exploring *Hypnagogia* – soon to be discussed.

Alejo: Okay.
Cathy: It's not a toenail clipper?
Alejo: WHY DID YOU SAY THAT?
Cathy: I don't know. It just came to mind.
Alejo: RIGHT NOW, I was imagining putting a toenail
clipper in my bag, to not forget it.

Mediumship

In a bereavement group for parents, *Bob and Phran Ginsberg* were gently, but firmly, informed that their attempts to discuss life continuing past death did not relate to coping with grief.

"We found that odd," says Bob, "as we believed that the only thing that could provide comfort to bereaved parents was the possibility that their child still survived."[18]

Intent on providing just such a forum, the Ginsbergs founded the Forever Family Foundation (FFF). I joined in 2010 and entered their Christmas Raffle in hopes of winning a reading with a certified medium. And I did. But that's not all.

Five months later, I entered their Earth Day Raffle and won **two of the five readings**. Up to this point in my life, I had won one raffle. In 1991. With Aaron. We won a book.

Readings: All three mediums *correctly* stated that:

- My son had crossed/passed **very** quickly.
- He had suffered a ferocious impact to his chest.
- He was physically impressive.
- He is very much a family man.
- He was entering a new field of study or work at the time of his crossing.
- He is a great lover of nature.
- He was proud of his teeth.

First Reading, with Angelina Diana
January 27, 2011:

Angelina began, "The first thing I am feeling is a younger energy coming through and they have a very spicy energy to them. Do you have a child who has passed?" **Yes.**

At 20:55:[i] "So he claims that you are honoring him through education. Is this true?" **Well, no.** "That's how he makes me feel. So for example, sometimes parents put together memorial scholarships, or they take on mentoring children in the same field–some aspect of the path that their child was physically going on. He gives me the feeling that this is something that you are doing now. Do you understand this?" **No.**

"Okay, well, he sees you doing this. He makes me feel when he looks back on it, there was an aspect of his energy that you are carrying on – when it comes to the education he was taking on – so he claims that you are honoring him.

Wait – WAS HE A BIG FOOTBALL FAN?" **Yes.** "He just threw a football when I said that." **Really?** "I have to honor the football connection to him. Do you understand this?" **YES!**

"Okay. Interesting. As I said that educational thing, he just whizzed the football past in front of my face and threw it. I want to honor – it has to be surrounded or connected to him."

Explanation of the Scholarships and the football connection: Aaron spent a lot of time with his Aunt Kim and his Uncle Brad as a child, as a teenager, and as an adult. On October 17, 2010, Brad told me that he was working on scholarships in Aaron's name that would begin in the fall of 2011. (I had not thought of Brad's scholarships as they were still nine months away.)

---

[i] This means 20 minutes and 55 seconds into the recorded reading.

Brad told me that he had made a plaque with a picture of Aaron in his high school football jersey (number 53) to put in the schools and the club where the scholarships were going to be offered. And Brad told me, "Aaron's number with me is 53. *Our connection is all about football*."

Angelina continued, and at 24:30: "Is there a Ma-call[i] connected to him? A Ma-call?" **No, nothing comes to mind.**

"If you could write that down or remember that part–he makes me feel like it is definitely connected to *sports or to the football connection – like it is very closely grounded to the football connection*." **Okay. I will write it down.**

I called Brad immediately after the reading to tell him what had been said about the scholarship and the football connection. He told me that he had sent the first scholarship check that very day, nine months ahead of schedule.

Brad could think of no Ma-call connected to his work for Aaron until I asked, "What is the name of that kid whose football jersey you got me?" **Brad answered, "Matt Cawl."**

---

[i] Angelina did **not** say *Michael*. She pronounced *Ma-call*. Repeatedly.

Explanation of Football Jersey: Aaron was raised in Iowa City, home of the Iowa Hawkeyes, and he and his Uncle Brad are fervent fans of the Hawks. In honor of Aaron, Brad had gotten a football signed by all of the Hawk players and managers. He had also arranged, in honor of Aaron, for me to receive a "number 53 jersey" that had been worn by a local boy when he played for the Hawks, and who then went on to play professionally. The name of the local boy and former owner of the jersey turns out to be Matt Kroel, but Brad had been pronouncing his name as **Matt Cawl** – exactly as Angelina pronounced it: Ma-call.

> **Brad's summary:** The medium could not have known about the football, or the jersey, or the scholarships. Not from Google or any other source. All these things were done in private, between me and other individuals just doing it. It was never in the paper, no publicity. Nothing. The medium would have had to call the players, or coaches, or the manager, or me, and that did not happen because it was all done in silence. I don't know what to make of it, but I do know there is no way anyone could have known Matt Cawl + Iowa football + Scholarships. No way. So the medium is legit.

Brad's words, "So the medium is legit" reminded me of William James'[i] famous quote, "If you wish to upset the law that all crows are black, you mustn't seek to show that no

---

[i] One of the most influential thinkers of all times, psychologist and philosopher William James is called the "Father of American Psychology." He founded both the modern school of psychology and the American Society for Psychical Research. His work, including his classic *The Varieties of Religious Experience: A Study in Human Nature,* is carefully studied worldwide, profoundly affecting all areas of investigation concerned with the mysteries of existence.

crows are; it is enough if you prove one single crow to be white." James was asserting his position that as soon as one medium is proven legitimate (in his case Leonora Piper), it could no longer be *reasonably* assumed that all mediums are frauds. Of course, the use of reason is never mandatory.

Second reading, with Dave Campbell
June 5, 2011:

Dave: "Who is the L name?" **Luke?** "I am not getting information on him." **It's a woman.** "Oh. I was getting nothing when thinking of a man. Yes, a woman, and a very strong personality. Real forceful. She was very much a perfectionist." **Yes.** I get her passing. She got really sick." **Yes.** "Like really weak. Like her whole personality changed and went inward. Like her body shut down. Hit her hard is what I am getting." **Yes.**

"She says that she is very grateful to you for helping her. I don't think you were exactly around her, but she says that you helped her a lot and she is very grateful for that."

What did I do that could have helped Sister Luke, other than having made the great effort with her to get beyond our inherited beliefs about death, before she died?

Third reading, with Laura Lynn Jackson
September 27, 2011

After explaining her procedure, the first words out of Laura Lynn's mouth were, "Okay. I have people stepping in already. Your dad has crossed, yes? I have a father figure on the other side. Your father has crossed right?" **Yes.** "On Dad's side of the family – is there a Richard?" **Yes.** "Okay, because I want to put a Richard[i] there. It's like BOOM – they're all coming through at once.

---

[i] There was *absolutely no hesitation* on Laura Lynn's part with my dad's name *Richard*.

It's like you've got quite a few people over there waiting to say hello to you." **Okay.** "They are also talking about someone in the family lost a child? Do you understand that?" **Yes.** "Okay. Does that – that goes to you yes?" **Yes.** "Okay, because they are pointing down to you. And, I also have a male on the other side. Do you understand this?" **Yes.** "Is this a son for you that crossed, yes?" **Yes.**

"And I have to say also that son is also with *Richard* on the other side. Is Richard like a grandfather figure?" **Yes.** "Richard had crossed before your son, yes?" **Yes.** "Okay. Somehow, I need to let you know that Richard helped him cross. I don't know if you prayed in a way or said can you guys help him or can someone take care of him? Do you understand this?" **Yes.**

"Because Richard stepped in. And I'm supposed to say he heard you." **Okay.** "Did you ask him directly to step in and help?" **Yes.** "Okay, because it is very, very important that I say like you are very, very connected on the other side, Cathy, whether or not you know it is a whole other thing.[i] I think that you do. When you say a prayer, when you make requests, they listen. They are there for you."

At 20:05: "Are you trying to get your husband to eat healthy? Your son is saying like lay off it. He is teasing you, but I don't know if *your husband* is – wait – I'm hearing "teddy" or "heddy." Wait. He is showing me a teddy bear.

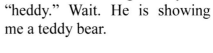

Husband and teddy bear: As part of our ongoing research, Alejo had drawn two images "for Aaron to get to me" which are shown at left. At the first mention of "your husband,"

---

[i] As are we all. Whether we know it or not.

Laura Lynn is shown one of the two images that Alejo had drawn. A Bear.

Laura Lynn continued, "Is there like a teddy bear like when he was younger of his that you still have?" **Yes.** "Is this by your room, by your bed? Did you *just* take it there?" **Yes.** "He is teasing you about that. It is somehow like ratty?" **Yes.** "He is joking with you about that."

Explanation: Aaron's dad, Joe Schaffer, gave me Cuddles as a Christmas gift when we were both fifteen years old, and I had given Cuddles to Aaron on his third birthday.

It is true that Cuddles is a bit ratty now, but he is still well loved. I had washed Cuddles and placed him on my pillow the week before the reading, just as Laura Lynn said.

Cuddles Joe Jensen.

Explanation (in advance) for Jason: Aaron's Aunt Ellen was grieving his death in that vulnerable way that "brings helpers." A woman approached her saying, "I know exactly what your sister is going through; tell her to call me if she feels like it."

I didn't want to talk to anyone, but, because Ellen thought it was important, I called the woman. We agreed to meet on the next Friday.

From my Walk-About Book, dated September 17, 2010:

I met Ana today and her daughter Karina. Her son Jason died in a car wreck. He was only 16. TODAY IS HIS BIRTHDAY. Ana carries his shirt with her everywhere she goes. She brought it into the coffee shop. People put things on "Jason's tree," close to where the accident happened. They beep their horns and blow kisses. Ellen and I will have to go by there. In their house, they have Jason's Wall and they put things on it. Ana said that people think they are crazy, but they don't care. I would like to see Jason's Wall. Ana told me that she knows exactly how I feel and to call her anytime. I'm glad I went.

At 22:45: Laura Lynn says, "I hear a J name. I want to go to a Jason. Is that somebody around him?" **Jason? No.** "Like a Jason or Janice? It's some J he is trying to reference. It's his peer group. I don't know if he has a cousin with a J name?" **No.** "It's like to his side a little bit so I want to say this is someone he's close to or connected to. I don't know where to go with that but I am supposed to acknowledge that."

At 32:00: Laura Lynn says, "I get something like, tell Jason I said hi. Who is Jason?" **I don't know.** "Maybe check on this. Who is this Jason? It's like, tell Jason I said hi. That is how I am hearing it, or, wait ...

What is he saying? Jason says hi? Wait. Jason says hi. Are you friends – are you like in a bereavement group with other parents that have lost children?" **No.** "That is the only thing I can–" **OH MY GOD YES! Yes! That makes sense.**

"Okay, because that is where I want to go with this – he is making – he is smiling and I am supposed to go to that and you will understand, he says. Okay, so pass that on."

I did understand. I have never belonged to a parental bereavement group of any kind. In fact, at this point I had talked to two women and two women only about our children dying before we did.

Both of these encounters turn out to be very important for the mission: Claudelle Tiederman, whose story is in Directive 8, and Jason's mom Ana, the year before, on Jason's birthday.

Hypnagogia

The state of consciousness while falling asleep and while waking up has a long research history as well as an interesting name. Actually, it has two names, but we will mostly use hypnagogia, [hip-*nuh*-**goh**-jia]. I had never heard of it, which would not surprise long-time investigator of consciousness Wilson Van Dusen, who says:

> That in the twentieth century one can describe events in common experiences such as the hypnagogic state and surprise people with its structure and contents seems almost beyond belief. Everyone has spent hundreds of hours in this state between sleeping and waking, yet it is largely unknown, but there it is. Our attention seems captured elsewhere by television, our labor and the many things of the world.[19]

Of course, Van Dusen is talking about common individuals like me. There is an illustrious community of inventors, artists, writers, scientists, mystics, and theologians who *intentionally* accessed (and access) hypnagogia with various goals in mind.

Highly decorated and internationally known Swedish inventor-scientist Emanuel Swedenborg[i] put himself into a state of receptivity that sounds a lot like hypnogogia in order to communicate with non-incarnate beings, as did Edgar Cayce and Rudolf Steiner.

Mary Shelley saw her famous *Frankenstein* in what she called a waking dream, and Robert Louis Stevenson is reported to have received *The Strange Case of Dr. Jekyll and Mr. Hyde* as he was waking up.

---

[i]At close to 60 years of age, Emanuel Swedenborg was improving his concentration by breathing minimally and focusing inwardly. He suddenly found himself wandering the state of consciousness where the dead live. He used his fine mind to investigate and communicate his discoveries, forever changing the everyday walk-about world.

Friedrich Kekule attributed his image of the benzene molecule to a daydream and his theory of the structure of atoms to a vision while dozing in a moving vehicle. Nikola Tesla stated, "My brain is only a receiver, in the Universe there is a core from which we obtain knowledge, strength, and inspiration. I have not penetrated into the secrets of this core, but I know that it exists." Seeing his contributions, one has to assume that he penetrated into that core of secrets after all.

Thomas Edison and Salvador Dali certainly did. They both intentionally accessed hypnagogia by holding something solid as they power-napped. If hypnagogia flowed into sleep, the solid objects would fall and startle them awake so that insights could be garnered. And used.

I knew nothing of hypnagogia, but I had a notebook full of events described as: *not quite awake, not quite asleep, kind of a vision, words I somehow felt, words I had to write down in the dark, words I was repeating as I woke up to not forget,* and *hearing words in the air.*

Mandaran Kanati: [Taken from my Walk-About Book] Deep in despair, I closed my eyes, and begged, "I need a new word for God; the old image gets in my way." **"MANDARAN KANATI"** came out of the air. It was clear. *I heard it."*

I was so shocked at having heard a voice in the air, that all I could do was document what had happened. Whatever it was.

The doors to the mysterious world of hypnagogia were opened by Gary Lachman's book, *A Secret History of Consciousness,* where I came across an experience with a familiar ring to it.

Celebrated researcher, lecturer, and author Julian Jaynes was in such turmoil at his inability to explain coherently how humans know anything at all, that he had to have a lie-down. In his own words:

My convictions and misgivings had been circling about through the sometimes precious fogs of epistemologies, finding nowhere to land. One afternoon I lay down in intellectual despair on a couch. Suddenly, out of an absolute quiet, there came a firm, distinct loud voice from my upper right, which said, "Include the knower in the known!" It lugged me to my feet absurdly exclaiming "Hello?" looking for whoever was in the room. The voice had had an exact location. No one was there! Not even behind the wall where I sheepishly looked. I do not take this nebulous profundity as divinely inspired, but I do think it is similar to what has been heard by those who in the past claimed such special selection."[20]

My heart raced and my breath caught when, having followed Lachman's advice to read *The Natural Depth in Man* by Wilson Van Dusen, I saw the beginning of an explanation of both my own nebulous profundity and that of Julian Jaynes:

Much of the hypnagogic area looks simply like cute images and odd sentences being tossed around in one's head until one asks precisely what the individual was *thinking of at that same moment. Then it begins to look like either a representation of the person's state or an answer to his query* [my italics].[21]

Three years after having heard "Mandaran Kanati" in the air, I was at a Yoga Conference with Kandy: I asked many yoga experts, "Do the words *Mandaran Kanati* mean anything to you?" One after another, the reply was, "No." The last presentation of the conference was *"What Happens After Death?"* Kandy and I almost didn't go, worried as we were that we might have to sit through another "whatever happens is for the best" lecture.

But no, there were people of all ages, in beautifully colorful clothing, singing, dancing, and handing out cookies. The swami laughed continuously while he gently poked fun at our everyday concerns. It was joyful.

When they finished, I ventured over to the group and stammered, "This might be strange, but I was sort of meditating and asked for a word for God, and I *heard* the words *Mandaran Kanati*. Do they mean anything to you?"

"Oh sure," the swami replied. "That is the mantra (**chant**) that we use. It is a gateway or portal to God. *Kanati* means "to make," so, put yourself in the center of the mandalas[i] and connect to God.

Give me your email address and I will send you the mandalas. So, this came to you in meditation. So very interesting."

For three years, I had been asking people to write down what, if anything, popped into their minds when they heard the words, *Mandaran Kanati*. Finally, my sister Christy's insight that it was a special **chant** for enlightenment could be woven into the emerging tapestry:

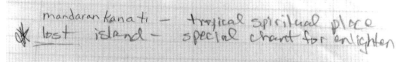

Christy's insight into Mandaran Kanati.

The promised mandalas did arrive a short time later, along with an email, a portion of which is given below:

Dear Cathy: *Hare Krishna!* *I'm the Swami that was at the Yoga's Congress in Elche. I hope that this letter met you very well by God's grace.

Remember the translation from Sanskrit and Malayam, of "mandalam karoti or mandaran karati" means: "Please concentrate and meditated in the mandala (or yantra)." Your friend,* Kesava Dasa Swami. Pranams. Namaste.

---

[i] *Mandala*: a graphic symbol of the universe often used as an aid to meditation.

Hypnopompia

Fredric Myers felt there was enough of a difference between hypnagogia, the state of consciousness while falling asleep, and the state of consciousness while waking up, that he coined a second term for the latter: hypnopompia.

Rudolf Steiner agrees, and he seems to know. His research[i] had led him to the conclusion that the best time to ask questions of the dead is while falling asleep, and the best time to be alert for their answers, which can be *audible* to more than one person, is while waking up.

Neither I, nor, it seems, Julian Jaynes, knew anything about hypnagogia or hypnopompia, so ignorance is obviously no block.[ii] Anyone interested in intentionally accessing these states of consciousness can consult the many practitioners who detail precise methods: Steiner and Van Dusen, for example.

Although different names are used for different methods, each is describing a way to learn a *mode of experiencing* Campbell's supernormal range of human spiritual life – including the range where the dead live.

Anyone who wants to learn this mode of experiencing can begin by disciplining herself to wake gently and become softly aware of what is on her mind ... and drowsily write it down, before waking consciousness takes over.

---

[i] A small sampling of Steiner's vast research that is particularly on topic: *Threshold of the Spiritual World; Staying Connected: How to Continue Your Relationships With Those Who Have Died; How to Know Higher Worlds: A Modern Path of Initiation; The Dead Are With Us; Intuitive Thinking as a Spiritual Path*; and *Mystics of the Renaissance*.

[ii] Andrea Mavromatis' thesis, *Hypnagogia: The Nature and Function of the Hypnagogic State*, submitted in 1983 to the Department of Psychology, Brunel University, for the degree of Doctor of Philosophy, has been a catalyst for much of the renewed interest in hypnagogia.

Peak Experiences

"Peak experience" is Abraham Maslow's term for events very similar to what I am calling opening-door events. He, and many others, have documented that peak experiences occur frequently to healthy individuals, under many different sorts of circumstances.

Ellen's peak experience/opening-door event: Talking to Ellen by phone, she suddenly screamed, "OH MY GOD! OH MY GOD!" I heard pure joy in her voice.

Ellen was collecting heart rocks for a garden she was creating for Aaron. On a stone that she had seen a hundred times before, the sacred something suddenly *showed itself to her* in the form of a small perfect heart with a teardrop etched on the rock. She **felt** it. She **knew**. Ellen wrote directly into my Walk-About Book, which is shown below:

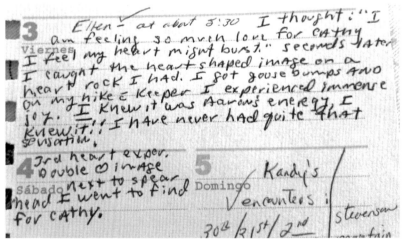

Her feelings expressed as, "I experienced immense joy. I **knew** it was Aaron's energy. **I knew** it!! I have never had quite that sensation," have been repeated, with different words, world-wide, by millions – every time the sacred something tries to make itself known.

Cosmic Consciousness

In the year 1872, Richard Maurice Bucke was on his way home in a horse-drawn carriage after having passed the evening pleasantly discussing poetry with two friends. In a state of what he calls a quiet, almost passive enjoyment, all at once, without any warning of any kind:

> ... there came upon him [Bucke documented his experience in the third person] a sense of exultation, of immense joyousness accompanied or immediately followed by an intellectual illumination quite impossible to describe. Into his brain streamed one momentary lightening-flash of the Brahmic Splendour which ever since lightened his life. Upon his heart fell one drop of the Brahmic Bliss, leaving thenceforward for always an aftertaste of Heaven.

> Among other things *he did not come to believe, he saw and knew* [my italics] that the Cosmos is not dead matter but a living Presence, that the soul of man is immortal, that the universe is so built and ordered that without any peradventure all things work together for the good of each and all, that the foundation principle of the world is what we call love and that the happiness of everyone is in the long run absolutely certain.[22]

Calling his experience his "initiation to the new and higher order of ideas," Bucke spent his remaining years seeking to understand his experience in rational terms, and gifted humanity with his Great and Holy Work, *Cosmic Consciousness: A Study in the Evolution of the Human Mind.*

In his book, Bucke presents a tri-layered model of consciousness, and proposes that progress from the first layer, Simple Consciousness, to the second layer, Human Self Consciousness, is more or less automatic. The third level, for which he popularized the term "Cosmic Consciousness" is a level of consciousness that he felt was accessed by few, and *understood and developed* by even fewer:

This consciousness shows the cosmos to consist not of dead matter governed by unconscious, rigid, and unintending law; it shows it on the contrary as entirely immaterial, entirely spiritual, and entirely alive; it shows that death is an absurdity, that everyone and everything has eternal life; it shows that the universe is God and that God is the universe, and that no evil ever did or ever will enter into it.[23]

Bucke is quick to point out that although much of what is described in Cosmic Consciousness seems absurd from the point of view of Self Consciousness, which is what he feels humanity's general level to be, it is nevertheless, "undoubtedly true."

To *know* that the experiences in Cosmic Consciousness are "undoubtedly true" requires *seeking*.

Which is exactly what Astronaut Edgar Mitchell did when his 1971 experience of Cosmic Consciousness so widened his vision, that walking on the moon was no longer seen to be out of this world:[i]

What I felt was an extraordinary personal connectedness. I experienced what has been described as an ecstasy of unity. I not only *saw* the connectedness, I *felt* it sentiently. I was overwhelmed with the sensation of physically and mentally extending out into the cosmos.[24]

Mitchell accepted the invitation from the sacred something that had shown itself to him, hung up his moon-walking boots,

---

[i] Mitchell tells us that, "This wasn't a "religious" or otherworldly experience, although many have tried to cast similar events in that mold. Nor was it a totally new scientific understanding of which I had suddenly become aware. It was just a pointer, a signpost showing the direction toward new viewpoints and greater understanding. The human being is part of a continuously evolving process, a more grand and intelligent process than classical science and the religious traditions have been able to correctly describe."

and co-founded the Institute for Noetic Sciences: a research institute for grasping opening-door events, peak experiences, and experiences of Cosmic Consciousness in rational terms.

Researcher Jenny Wade beautifully articulates (with different terminology) the importance of *investigating, understanding, and developing* not only experiences of Cosmic Consciousness, but all opening-door events.

In her book, *Changes of Mind: A Holonomic Theory of the Evolution of Consciousness* she presents a model of consciousness as a spectrum, stretching from what she calls "Pre- and Perinatal Consciousness" through "After-Death Consciousness." Wade proposes that progress from a more restricted rung of consciousness to a more expansive rung depends on how one meets a *crisis of understanding.*

A "crisis of understanding" is a glimpse of reality beyond one's current position on the spectrum of consciousness.

Most crises of understanding are painful *because they challenge one's core beliefs with all of the underlying assumptions.*[i]

Opening-door events and peak experiences can be somewhat different, as they come with an immense joy and a total sureness that Life is much more than a body that ends in death. But the sureness cannot last if one's beliefs forbid the existence of what just happened.

If one does not work to enlarge understanding beyond the beliefs that define each level or rung of consciousness, the crisis of understanding will be denied, dismissed, forgotten, and wasted.

---

[i] Wade provides a useful summary of common "transition dilemmas" (i.e., crises of understanding) that challenge the *beliefs that define each stage or rung of consciousness.*

After a while, it is as if these experiences never happened at all. In the words of Colin Wilson:

> Every surge of "contemplative objectivity" shows the mind its own ability to grasp reality by reaching out. The only way to acquire a skill is to keep repeating the attempt until you have learned the knack. Now, it is true that most healthy people have "peak experiences" fairly often. *But they fail to make a determined effort to build on them* [my italics]. They take them for granted, and allow themselves to slip back into their dull, non-expectant state of mind, the old plodding attitude towards existence.[25]

How would anyone make a determined effort to build on crises of understanding? By investigating and developing them. That is, by seeking to understand them in rational terms.

Why would anyone bother to do this? Because seeking to understand these types of experiences increases both their frequency and their quality.

And it is the frequency and quality of the experiences, combined with the effort to understand them that *evolves consciousness.*

This is the Great and Holy Work. And it is assigned to each and every one of us. Dead and Alive.

The crises of understanding that I have been calling opening-door events are *unorthodox invitations* to join The Work, addressed by the invisible hands of the dead. That is the hypothesis. The data follows.

Directive 8: Accept your Invitations to Further the Evolution of Consciousness

"The immense fulfillment of the friendship between those engaged in furthering the evolution of consciousness has a quality impossible to describe."
—Pierre Teilhard de Chardin

Everyone receives unorthodox invitations from the dead to further the evolution of consciousness. It's just they are not always easy to recognize, arriving as they do in a discontinuous, non-linear fashion.

Each piece of each invitation is a gossamer thread[i] for a tapestry that becomes clear *only if it gets woven*. And YOU are the weaver. Here are two examples:

Invitation One – First Thread: I was in a Celtic shop with two of my nieces and decided to draw a card from the packs of tarot cards placed around the store.

I drew a card *from the middle* of two different stacks, and, both times, I drew *"Wait for the Invitation."* But that's not all.

That evening the three of us went to discuss opening-door events with "an intuitive." Upon arrival, I was told, "I came across a new thing on the net that looked like fun and for some reason I put your information.

Catherine Jane Jensen

Type: Projector

Signature: Success

Not-Self Theme: Bitterness

Inner Authority: Emotional Authority

Strategy: Wait for the Invitation

Incarnation Cross: Left Angle Cross of The Alpha

For what it's worth, your strategy should be to *Wait for the Invitation."* **CLICK. *All three of us felt it.***

---

[i] From Walt Whitman's poem, *A Noiseless Patient Spider.*

I assumed that "wait for the invitation" was a message for the material world telling me that if I couldn't buck up, at least I should shut up – until invited to share. This interpretation simmered uneasily for about four years, until I met a minister with very different ideas about who invites whom to do what.

The Second Thread was flung by my brother Greg and sister-in-law Ann when they asked me to show them the game-like activities for "normalizing conversation about collaboration with the dead" that were busily birthing themselves in my dreams.

Greg was a very enthusiastic player and told me, "Cathy! You were born to do this! But not so much in grief retreat sort of places. I think you should try to find junior colleges or churches that will invite you to give these workshops."

Twenty minutes later, I was walking down a wooded road. A car stopped and Helen introduced herself. She mentioned that she had to get along as she and some others were moving James Stacey, their new pastor. New pastor, eh? Greg did mention being invited by a church ...

I went with Helen and soon met Deb and Lee. All three were members of a congregation called Unity. I had no idea what Unity was. I thought it was Unitarian, which I had no idea about either. Lee mentioned that their study group was reading *The Four Agreements* by Miguel Ruiz. "Hmm," I thought. "Interesting book for a church group to be discussing." Ann agreed, and that very night we visited the Unity church in Sunrise Beach, Missouri.

The Third Thread was Pastor James Stacey's welcoming Ann and me with a prayer card quoting *Rudolf Steiner!* *CLICK*. I had been studying Steiner for three years and had *longed* for a chance to discuss his ideas. Until now, no one I knew had even heard of him.

I asked Pastor Stacey for an appointment. When we met, I shared with him what I felt was my most compelling evidence that I was part of a mission to encourage collaboration between the living and the dead.

I finished by saying, "Only forty-eight hours ago, my brother suggested that I find churches to host my workshops; when you gave me the quote from Steiner, I thought maybe your church was the one." "Of course it is," Pastor Stacey replied. "The world is one spirit. The dead do want to work with us. They *invite* us. Steiner talks being *invited* by spiritual beings to work with them. I have been wanting to do something that approaches death differently. This can be a good way to get started. Yes. Please do offer your special classes here."

 ## DEATH

The one sure thing in this life is
rarely a welcomed topic of
conversation.

Faith and/or hope of a future reunion might console others,
but will not do for consoling ourselves.
Proof is what we need.

PROOF of what?
That death is not a dead end.

Is death at all *knowable*? Now? Before we die? What is there to be explored and where could we start? Please join us to consider these questions and more as we work our way though games/activities designed to *bring our individual assumptions about death* into the light for a careful look. Invitation open to all.

- Absolutely no religious affiliation.
- Absolutely no dogmas. No right. No wrong.
- Absolutely no belief systems parading as fact, whether they be called religious or said to be scientific.

Simply a shared effort at extending vision for a better understanding.

Place: Graciously offered by Unity at the Lake Church, Sunrise Beach, Missouri
Date: February 22, 2015
Time: 12:30 - 3:00 p.m.
Fee: Open minded interest.
Thanantologist: Cathy Jensen de Sánchez. Elche, Spain

Materials provided
Contact: www.mission7255.net

I made the flyer shown above, and, four months later, a group of us gathered in friendship to engage in the furthering of the evolution of consciousness.

Invitation Two – First Thread: Rosamond Lehmann wrote a very beautiful testimony of her journey into the realm of the dead in search of her daughter, Sally. Every time I read her *Swan in the Evening: Fragments of an Inner Life*, things would focus a bit more, as her words so clearly stated my blurry condition in what used to be my straightforward walkabout world:

> I was unable either to remain appropriately dumb or speak out steadily about my new knowledge and my investigations; and consequently I was **racked by a sense of doubly betraying the loved and vanished child**; [emphasis added] and was doubtless felt to be very awkward socially when, lacerated almost beyond bearing, I strove and stammered to explain why the idea of distraction, or of change of scene – those vain panaceas recommended to all mourners – was odious to me.[26]

In her book, Rosamond mentions, very briefly, a German God by the name of *Wotan*. Although I had never heard of *Wotan*, he seemed oddly familiar. He stayed strongly on my mind.

The Second Thread was flung by my own hand. Buying groceries, I was compelled to talk to a fellow shopper who was tattooed from head to toe. I explained my impertinence by telling him that his tattoos reminded me of my nephew Leif Eric; that my son had just died; and that I felt I needed to know the story he was wearing on his body.

His tattoos, he told me, speak of a *wandering* God named Odin who facilitates communication between the living and the dead. The stranger finished by saying, "He is called *Wotan* in German." I felt dizzy. I clutched the man. I hung on to him so that I wouldn't fall. Right then and there I claimed **Odin** in his aspect of a **Wandering**[i] God of Communication between the Living and the Dead for help on my quest to find Aaron.

---

[i] I had claimed *wanderer* as a personal symbol way back in 1984. With this information, Wotan's strange familiarity resolved itself.

Dustin Smith Jensen is the **Third Thread**. Aaron and Dustin are not related, although their mothers have the same family name and the boys called each other "brother."

The first thing Aaron told me when I got off the plane in Spain on April 4, 2010 was, "Mom! Dustin and I hooked up!"

Many years had passed since their shared classes in Eastern Religions, their long nights philosophizing, and their sincere efforts to highlight the similarities of humanity's wisdom traditions by making an Esperanto-type book of Sacred Scriptures.

Dustin has long been a seeker deeply motivated to comprehend the great mysteries of existence. His authentic interest, his extensive knowledge,[i] and his open sharing of experiences have been instrumental in the work of the Aaron Schaffer Jensen Family Foundation.

One fine day I asked Dustin about the figure that comes with his emails. He replied, "That is a Nordic God who is so familiar in my household that my daughter Lily thinks of him as a grandfather. His name is *ODIN*." **CLICK**. I had to lie down.

---

[i] Dustin's websites: (https://www.scienceabbey.com/2018/04/14/the-christian-journey/) (https://www.royalartsociety.com/2017/09/05/ancient-conceptions-of-spirit-and-deity/)

The Fourth Thread was flung by my friend Claudelle Tiederman, after her death.

In August of 2010, Claudelle and I tried to help each other process the fact that *our* children could die before we did.

Shockingly, four years later I was attending Claudelle's Celebration of Life where I felt her personal symbol vibrating with such meaning that, with no awareness of how or where to use it, I asked for permission to incorporate it into the work of the foundation.

Neither was there any awareness that the date of her celebration, **October 26,** was a gossamer thread. Not by any of the so-called living anyway.

It took years to weave Claudelle's threads into the burgeoning tapestry, but in 2015 things began when her symbol was used for the flyer announcing that first AlmaOde[i] Workshop, held at the Unity church in Missouri. Claudelle's symbol is also used in the directory to indicate that "collaboration with the dead has been recognized." As you will see.

The Fifth Thread was a seemingly simple invitation to go for a walk with my friend Carina. On **October 26.** It soon became apparent that it was not so simple, after all.

---

[i] AlmaOde is an acronym for Aaron's Living Matrix Alliance, Opening-Door Events. *Alma* is Spanish for soul, and *Ode* you already know.

Although I had been spending much time with her and her husband Rodrigo, **October 26** was the day that Carina decided to tell me that her sister Lili had left the physical realm only ten months ago. That night I had a vivid dream:

A woman says to me, "Can you wake my husband up? He is not a morning person."

When I asked if her husband was grouchy, she answered, "He's Spanish."

"Oh," I said. "I have had plenty of experience with that!"

Her husband was in a coffin. As I was pulling off the lid, I asked the woman, "What's his name?"

"Hideón," she answered.

I asked in Spanish, "Hideón con (with) H?" I began to call his name. "Hideón, wake up! Hideón, wake up!" He began to open his eyes and then, he sat up. All the while I kept saying, "Buenos días Hideón! Buenos días!"

Waking up, I heard myself repeating, "Hideón, like Hideous. Hideón like Hideous" – to remember the name.

Researching **Hideón**, I was led to the word *hȳdan* and three ancient texts: *Beowolf*, *Wladere*, and **Wanderer**.

What is **Wanderer**? A tale of a wandering hero who discovers the meaning of life. How does he proceed? By struggling to understand the opening-door events that came with death.

This was too much for one mind to carry, and a group of us accepted our unorthodox invitations to gather in friendship and do our best to engage in the furthering of the evolution of consciousness.

Threads for Weaving the Tapestry

Odin:
- I had claimed *wanderer* as a personal symbol in 1984.

- I claimed Odin's aspect as a *Wandering* God of Communication between the living and the dead via Rosamond Lehman's book about seeking her physically dead daughter Sally.

- Dustin, Aaron's brother in the work of furthering the evolution of consciousness, lives in Jakarta, where Rosamond's Sally died.

- Dustin claims Odin as a personal symbol.

The Date of October 26 is:
- Dustin's birthday.

- The date of Claudelle's celebration of life, where the AlmaOde symbol was recognized and claimed.

- The date on which, eighteen years *before* Claudelle's celebration, the heart of the first recipient of her symbol, stopped beating. (To be explained shortly.)

- The date that Hideón demonstrated that if you call to those who believe themselves dead, at least some of them will wake up.

- The date that Carina introduced her sister **Lili.**

Lily, Lili, and Lilies:
- Carina's sister is Lili.

- Odin's flower is a Lily, although Dustin and his wife Renny didn't know that when they named their daughter **Lily**.

- Aaron's **lilies** are the catalyst for becoming aware of how the *Directory* works, as you will soon see.

As our gathering was ending, Rodrigo shared a story: "When Facundo Cabral's[i] wife and baby were killed, Mother Teresa asked him what he would do with so much love. She didn't ask him what he would do with so much pain and sorrow," Rodrigo stressed. "But *what would he do with so much love.*" On that beautiful note, we all went home.

Carina and Rodrigo "weaving" at the gathering.

Alejo and I were entering our apartment when his cell phone sounded with an incoming message, which he checked. His voice was puzzled when he said, "Cathy, come here a minute. I don't know how any of this works, but, just look at this."

He showed me his screen: there was the same Facundo Cabral who had ended our gathering in such a meaningful way only a few minutes earlier.

---

[i] Argentine poet, musician, philosopher, and UNESCO Messenger of Peace Facundo Cabral stated that his spiritual views were influenced by a variety of figures, including Jesus, Jiddu Krishnamurti, Gautama Buddha, Schopenhauer, John the Baptist, Francis of Assisi, Gandhi, and Mother Teresa. He preached quantum mysticism and the subjugation of the ego.

The message had arrived right on time: Aniceto's 22:22.[i]

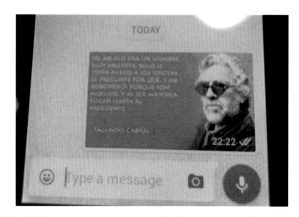

Humankind becomes aware of the sacred because it (the sacred) *shows itself to us*. We are repeatedly invited, beckoned, and, at times, almost begged, to become aware of the *mystery of the mysteries of existence **wanting** to be known.*

If you accept your opening-door events as invitations to learn, you will continuously document, search, research, and model-up. If you keep at it, you will come to *know* (not believe) that death is not a dead end. You might decide to stop there, which is fine.

Or, you might decide to collaborate with the dead on the Great and Holy Work of furthering the evolution of consciousness. Which is even better.

---

[i] We found out the next day that Alejo's friend, Juan, had sent the message three days earlier.

Directive 9: Collaborate with the Dead

"I want you to make a directory and put everybody's names,
and put them in contact with each other."
–Aaron Schaffer Jensen

Although the psyche is as unexplored as the hills of Mars, we toss psychological jargon back and forth like child's play. We think we know what we are talking about, but we do not. In the words of Carl Jung:

> It is a remarkable fact which we come across again and again, that absolutely everybody, even the most unqualified layman, thinks he knows all about psychology as though the psyche were something that enjoyed the most universal understanding. But anyone who really knows the human psyche will agree with me when I say that it is one of the darkest and most mysterious regions of our experience.[27]

The mysterious experience of the human *psyche* called thought (not to be confused as an activity initiated by and limited to the brain) is complicated when you stop to think about it.

So complicated that some of the best thinkers of every age have wondered what they were doing when they were thinking. Or, even if it (thinking) could be called a *doing* at all.

Most of it (thinking) seems to be less a *doing something* than a *something that is done*. The vast majority of it (thinking) is an automated process of labeling whatever fires our senses. This requires no thought at all.

In addition to robotically labeling sensory input, most of us thoughtlessly distract ourselves by rewording old stories, fine-tuning our tales of how things went wrong, anxiously imagining future solutions to anxiously imagined future predicaments, and in general just chatting over nothing at all, with ourselves.

This "monkey-mind activity" can be transcended by what many are now calling "focusing on the now," or "staying present." This is modern wording for an idea with a very long history.[i] And it really works. You can feel the difference. It feels like a relief.

Then there is what we call *intuitive thought*. This is a type of received or perceived thought which is only possible when the mechanized activity mentioned above is shocked into silence, or muted by the diligent practice of a meditative discipline aimed at shutting ourselves up.

Although the source of intuitive or perceived thought remains a mystery, the hypothesis is here put forward that much of it comes from the dead. In particular: from the dead who are engaged in furthering the evolution of consciousness.

Evidence supporting this hypothesis might not shock those growing up with the post-Newtonian model of reality which proposes that consciousness *is* before matter *becomes*. But it is still quite a jolt for those of us caught in the last vestiges of material realism.[ii]

Dates are included in the small sampling of evidence that follows only to demonstrate that (1) dates can become centers around which events gather and (2) much time can pass between a thread being flung and your ability to weave it in. If the dates make you dizzy, ignore them.

---

[i] A very small sampling: Plotinus, Jesus, Meister Eckhart, Paramahansa Yogananda, *A Course in Miracles*, B. K. S. Iyengar, Erwin Schrödinger and Eckart Tolle.

[ii] The basic tenet of material realism is, as has been mentioned ad nauseam no doubt, that matter (brain) produces consciousness. This belief has led a centuries-long quest to find the smallest piece of matter to see how it comes alive. But it just ain't so. Matter is a material that consciousness uses, but matter is not what *lives*. Consciousness is.

Ana Victoria was hurrying to get out of the pouring rain when she walked behind a van she assumed was parked. When the driver backed up, Ana was killed, instantly.

I met her daughter Gloria four months later, who told me that for the five nights following their mother's death, all eight siblings slept in the same room. During this time, Gloria dreamed with their mom, who explained that the driver had not seen her in the rain and didn't realize that he had hit her. Gloria said the dream helped everyone.

March 12, 2014: Two days after meeting Gloria, the intuition came to me to give her some of Aaron's Easter Lilies[i] for her mom's rosary.[ii] I gathered a huge bouquet of the flowers and dug up eight bulbs, one for each of Ana's children. I headed to the rosary at Gloria's.

Gloria was awe-struck. "This morning," she said, "I went to four different places to get these very flowers for my mom, but there weren't any. *My mom and your Aaron are connected, and they want us to know.*"[iii]

Entering her words into a small notebook where I kept birth and death dates, I *heard* Aaron's instructions, "I want you to make a directory and put everybody's names, and put them in contact with each other." **Oh my God! This is the directory.**

---

[i] Aaron planted these lilies for my Mother's Day gift in 2005.

[ii] In Venezuela, family and friends come and go from the home of the person who has died for nine straight days and nine straight nights to pray rosaries and grieve together. Gatherings are continued on the monthly anniversary of the death for the next six months, then yearly.

[iii] Gloria's theory, that Aaron and her mother had collaborated and sent the same intuition to both of us, worked its way through my pathologies of knowing and learning slowly but surely. I emphasize *slowly*. Don't get discouraged. Things/thoughts simmer below the surface for months, or even years, until your understanding enlarges (your consciousness evolves) and then, suddenly, miracles and magic are redefined.

Ana and Joaquin: Alejo and I left Venezuela to live in Spain. To get to know our neighbors, Alejo was frequenting "Ana's Cafe," but I rarely went. And when I did, I never chatted. I knew nothing about the regulars except that they had all grown up together and that the owner's [Ana] husband had died years ago. For some reason, July 26, 2014 was different.

I saw Ana across the street, and I hollered to her to wait for me. I asked all about her husband. What is his name? His birthday? When did he die? What happened? Ana answered all of my questions and asked one of her own: "Why all of the questions *today?*"

I stuttered and stammered about getting messages from Aaron, Aniceto, and my dad, about staying alert for numbers and dates, and about the importance of documenting. Sharing my unusual behavior with Alejo, he wondered, "Could today be Joaquin's Saint's Day?" YES. July 26 is a shared Saint's Day[i] for Ana and Joaquin.

Notes from the Directory.

---

[i]In general, a Saint's Day is more celebrated in Spain than a birthday, regardless of belief/non-belief in saints.

Ana was not impressed by what she called the curious co-incidence of my inquiring about Joaquin on his Saint's Day, but his daughter Cristina was. Because Joaquin was born on April 13 and left on February 13, Cristina said she would stay alert for the possibility of claiming 13 as her dad's number.

Ana's favorite uncle: Two years later Ana stopped me as I walked by her cafe. Noticeably troubled, she said, "Cathy, since you know about death, I need to talk to you. My uncle is dying. I should take my mom to see him, but she doesn't even know that her brother is sick. Maybe it would be too much for her?" Of course, it was actually too much for Ana, as it is often too much for most of us.

I did my best to share what little I knew, and told Ana that I would light a candle for her family, which I did. Her uncle died that day.

About two weeks later, I became aware of an intuition that the number 24 (in particular June 24) was important. To someone.

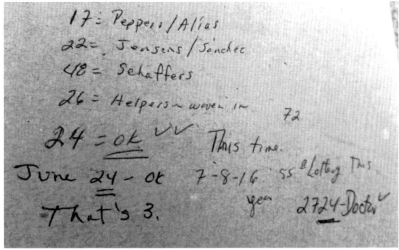

Trying to grasp the 24 intuition.

That someone seemed to be Ana's uncle. I told Alejo that I was getting an intuition that 24, in particular June 24, was connected to Ana's uncle. And I wrote it down in my Walk-About Book. Just in case.

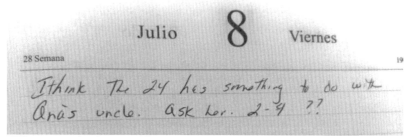

> Julio **8** Viernes
>
> 28 Semana   19
>
> *I think the 24 has something to do with Ana's uncle. Ask her. 2-4 ??*

When I asked Ana if June 24 had anything to do with her uncle, she started to cry. It is his Saint's Day. Ana confided to Alejo that she didn't understand how her uncle could have influenced me to tell her, yet …

Ana and I set a time to get together to try one of the "game-like activities for normalizing conversation about collaboration with the dead" that had worked well in the workshop. Ana even said she was going to bring her mother. But we were not fast enough. Ana stumbled over a truth, but then, she (literally) slept through the appointment.

Thinking that the use of the Saint's Day could be connected to Joaquin, I called his daughter Cristina. She said that yes, she certainly did want to hear all about it, and we made an appointment. But then, one week later, she also cancelled.

There are muted voices whispering our names, delivering assignments to us all in various times.[i] To not collaborate with those whispering, and then conclude that collaboration does not happen, is not only refusing your call to your high adventure, it is closing the door on your dead.

---

[i] From Ray Kinsella, who wrote the book *Shoeless Joe*, on which the movie *Field of Dreams* is based.

The Jacobsons: In Iowa, driving east on Interstate 80, I saw a sign for the Danish Windmill in Elkhorn. Suddenly *go there* came to my mind. STRONGLY:

"Go to the museum."
"No, don't go. It's getting late."
"Yes, go. Something important might be there."
"No, go straight to Kim's." I argued with – myself?

I passed the museum exit and then had to backtrack. Once inside the museum I thought I heard my Aunt Karen, but it turned out to be a woman named Deb. Right off, just in case, I told her and the girl working with her behind the counter, "How very strange. Somehow, I felt compelled to come to the museum. I wonder why."

I asked them if they knew my brother and sister-in-law, who taught there for a few years in the early 80's. Yes, Deb remembered them.

Then, for some reason, I asked Deb to write her name on a piece of paper. While doing so, she mentioned, "My name was different then. My husband Dean died." DING! DING! DING! I was instantly alert.

Deb explained: "Dean and our son Chad went on a long bicycle trip for Chad's 30th birthday. We had planned a family get-together at my cousin's house to celebrate Chad's birthday and their having completed their long ride. We all got there, and then – Dean's heart just stopped beating."

"Oh, GOD," my voice broke. "My son, too. Aaron's heart just stopped beating. Just all of a sudden. He just… DIED. Maybe that's it. Maybe that is why I had to come here." Deb and I started crying, and the girl behind the counter brought us tissues and joined in.

As I was leaving, a thought came to me; I turned and asked Deb,

"When is Dean's birthday?"

"November third," she replied.

"That's Aaron's birthday, too." **Click. We all felt it.**

Kim wondered if Deb's Dean (Jacobson) could be related to Greg and Ann's very close friend Joel (Jacobson). Yes. Dean and Joel are first cousins.

For some reason, I felt that Deb should know that Dean's first cousin is a very dear friend of my brother's family. When I called the museum, I was surprised to be told, "Deb's not here. She never works on Sundays."

Insisting that I had just talked to her three hours ago, right there in the museum, they rounded her up. "It's true," Deb said. "I never work Sundays. I just felt like coming in today."

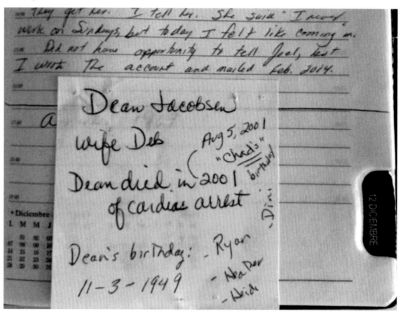

Notes from my Walk-About Book.

At least some of what we call intuition is the soft-spoken voices of the dead, in this case whispering to a woman to go to work on her day off, while whispering to another woman to stop in a museum because something important might be there.

Why would the dead do this? Couldn't Aaron's instructions to "put the living and the dead in contact with each other" *be a recruiting method for the great and holy work of furthering the evolution of consciousness?*

This hypothesis certainly seems to accommodate the data. The success or failure of the method hinges, of course, on whether the "living" members of the "dead" person's family *participate, investigate, and collaborate.*

Kathy, George, and Travis: My friend Kathy's son, Travis, left the physical realm the day before his birthday five years before I met her. She told me that both she and Travis' father, George, knew that death did not end a relationship, but, neither of them had gotten any sort of message from their son.

I wrote Travis' name and dates on a piece of paper for the directory.

Three months later, as I was getting ready to go to the Unity Church, for some reason I felt a need to look through the directory. Travis' piece of paper fell out. "Travis? Who is Travis?" I asked myself.

I did not remember him and I felt unhappy, careless, and regretful all the way to the Unity Church.

Once there, Kathy caught my arm, and, with a meaningful look and tone, she said, "This morning as I was waking up I heard, 'MOM! MOM!' I *heard* it Cathy. It was not a dream. I know it was Travis!"

Ah ha! Travis! There you are! I told Kathy that he had called for my attention that very morning – not more than thirty minutes ago. George listened silently, not saying a word.

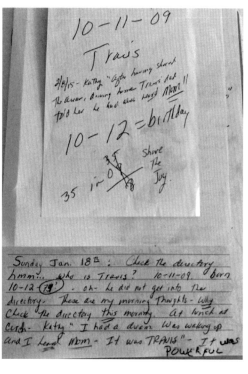

Next Sunday, Kathy took me aside and said, "Driving home last Sunday, George told me that he also *heard* Travis' voice calling 'MOM!'"

Two people waking up (in the state of consciousness known as hypnopompia) hear the voices of the dead calling out the same words. Just as Steiner, and many others, have carefully documented.

Karen and Larry Bailey: Karen Bailey is the dear friend who woke up at 2:22 a.m., and *knew* that the 2:22 was somehow connected to "those trying to help us," previously reported in the section about Aniceto and his number - 22.

This is Karen's story of engaging in the furthering of the evolution of consciousness – or this part of it anyway.

Karen and her father Larry entered our lives in 1987, when Karen was fifteen. I have loved her like a daughter from the moment I met her. Raised by Larry with much love and tender concern, Karen was devastated when he died of sudden cardiac arrest.

I had long wanted to contact her about Aaron, but each time I imagined the words coming out of my mouth, it hurt too much. I couldn't do it.

Then, on December 30, 2014, I dreamed with Larry Bailey, who told me, five times, to contact Karen. I called her the next day with the message from her dad. The re-connection was immediate, and Karen joined the Work.

Karen's message about 222 being important is now shown to the right in its entirety.

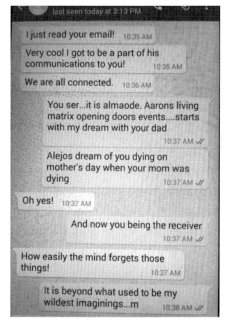

Let me explain: A year before Karen sent her message, Alejo had had a very upsetting dream. On *Mother's Day*,

In his dream, Karen was dying. She was lying with her head in Alejo's lap, and he was stroking her hair, trying to comfort her as they reminisced about our adventures as she and Aaron were growing up in Iowa City.

The dream worried Alejo and he insisted that I contact Karen. I did so – repeatedly, but heard nothing back.

Finally, I wrote to her, explaining that on *Mother's Day* Alejo had had a dream about her, and we wanted to be sure that she was okay. Karen responded immediately. She had been out of touch she said, because she was at her *mother's funeral*.

Karen is right: the mind does so easily forget these things. Unless "these things" are documented. She is also right that we are *ALL* connected, and this ALL includes those of the dead who are capable of passing their thoughts from mind to mind.[i]

Grandpa Jensen: I had a picture of my grandparents' farm for 8 years before I finally had it framed. I hung it on a **May 22.**

This got me to reminiscing, and, as I looked through the Directory for family dates, I was very surprised to see that I didn't have Grandpa Jensen's birthday. I felt VERY pushed to find it. I looked here and I looked there; I called this one and I asked that one, and then I emailed an aunt and asked her: "When is Grandpa's birthday?" **May 22,** was her reply.

"OH MY GOSH," I wrote back enthusiastically. "I hung the farm picture on May 22! Then I felt pushed to find Grandpa's birthday; he wants us to know he is here!"

I never heard back from my aunt, which is often how it goes, but Kim did hear back from Grandpa, two days later. It all began with the message at right.

> Thats cool. Did you read this morning at 522   9:48 AI
>
> Your first message that you sent last night was 522 here. You sent it at 1022 last night...or oh my god 2222 for the time here..   9:55 AM
>
> They use here that system of 1 pm is 1300.....   9:56 AM
>
> So you sent me the page from Leif book at 2222 your time...   9:56 AM

Kim's message (above) is referencing a page from *Zohar,* a book that her son Leif was using in his class on the Hebrew

---

[i] While writing this, I heeded an intuition to look at my baptismal certificate: I was baptized February 13 – Karen's father's birthday. The certificate was issued June 8 – Karen's mother's birthday.

mystical[i] system of Kabbalah. Our messaging was full of 22s, and we knew to be alert to the possibility of a message from the so-called dead.

The next morning, Kim sent the message at right, and 5:22 was brought into focus.

> Ok. At 5:22 am, i was awack-
> ened to the sound of someone
> screaming. It was so real, i
> thought it was gabe because
> baxter has been sick. Then i
> thought maybe the neighbor?
> Idk if it was in my dream but we

When the intuition to check the directory "got in," we recognized that 5:22 was not a time, but a DATE: Grandpa Jensen's birthday.

> That would make sense. So, his bday is may 22? Too cool if hes communicating with me or thriugh me 8:58 AM

< Kim's conclusion. Too cool indeed.

But, again, we might well ask, *"What's it all for?"* Are the dead really *just* saying, "Hello. I'm here. Be happy. See you when you die," as I have been told too many times to count?

That people are so nonchalant about the dead communicating absolutely blows my mind.

Anyone who is not shocked by communication from the dead does not understand what it means. It reminds me of a quote attributed to Niels Bohr:[ii] "Anyone who is not shocked by quantum theory has not understood it."

---

[i] *Mystical:* In material realism's model, "mystical" is a euphemism for "not real." In the current Post-Newtonian model, "mystical" is a euphemism for "not well understood." Mystically enough, Leif spoke recognizable Hebrew in his class – a language completely unknown to him.

[ii] Danish physicist Bohr received the 1922 Nobel Prize in Physics. Einstein accused Bohr of introducing mysticism into science and Bohr accused Einstein of misunderstanding his ideas.

No one can deny that receiving messages from loved ones who have died brings some comfort to broken hearts, but that's not all there is to it.

What I am calling opening-door events are the dead *wanting their presence known.* This presents a definite crisis of understanding for most of us.

The struggle to understand experiences of collaboration with the dead and to integrate them into your worldview is called seeking, and it is **your** seeking that expands **your** vision and enlarges **your** understanding of the nature of things,[i] i.e., **your** seeking evolves **your** consciousness.

This is the same struggle, with the same outcome – if the endeavor is sustained to completion – as what has been called, among other things:

- Nurturing spiritual growth.

- Learning or finding a mode to experience the supernormal range of human spiritual life.

- An alchemic process of transformation.

- A process of individuation.

- Engaging in the furthering the evolution of consciousness.

- A self-guided process of inner transformation.

- Learning the mysteries of existence.

Collaboration with the dead is another method that works. If you refuse to heed the trumpet calling you to your high adventure of collaborating with the dead, the *experiencing* of

---

[i] There are many options for greeting a crisis of understanding that challenges core beliefs besides evolving consciousness, e.g., denial, regression, dismissal, forgetting, etc. To choose to seek beyond one's beliefs is a deed of a spiritual hero.

consciousness continuing past death will, most likely, either be discarded as impossible, or remain only a *belief.* And beliefs are precariously fragile vehicles of truth.

If you *do* heed your trumpet call and begin your seeking, the day will come when you realize this is much too important to keep to yourself. But speaking out about it is not easy.

For many, talking about "collaboration with the dead" is a step beyond "inappropriate." It is just plain nuts.

At some point though, sheepish acquiescence to the culturally sanctioned, horribly self-destructive rule of keeping our mouths shut about death will no longer be an option, and the last task of the hero journey will begin. You will speak out.

Directive 10: Speak Out

*"If you cannot – in the long run – tell everyone what you have
been doing, your doing has been worthless."*
–Erwin Schrodinger

Collaboration with the dead is as common as the common cold, yet it is rarely mentioned. It is more important than the daily forecast, yet it is never covered on the six o'clock news. It is far more vital to our well-being than the statistics of our favorite sports teams or the growth of our investments, yet it is rarely, if ever, discussed. Why is this? How can this be?

According to Wilson Van Duesen, it is because humans don't know what is most natural to us:

> We seem mostly unconscious, like wordy fools, barely able to remember what we have said, and with almost no idea how words themselves arise. All this is to say that it is amazing how little of human experience is actually known. We seem to know far more of rocks, clouds, and machines *than we do of our own experiencing* [my italics].[28]

The directives are a method of becoming familiar with your own experiencing in the wild, super-normal range of human spiritual life where the dead live. As you speak out about your experiences, you normalize the conversation about life after death and encourage others to be open to their "soon to come" opening-door events.

Things resonate. And so does consciousness. In the same way that clock pendulums will slowly, but surely, end up swinging together, speaking out about opening-door events generates a field of receptivity that "pulls in" more and more events of ever-increasing complexity and quality.

As has been extensively documented: "If you build it, he/they will come."

Share the Stories: On Aaron's July 2 of 2017, my friends Carina, Rodrigo, their son Fernando, and I lit candles by the ocean and connected with our loved ones living in the non-physical realm of life. Long into that starlit night, we talked of this beautifully mysterious walk about world.

We shared our personal excursions into the range of human spiritual life where the dead live, as well as the excursions that our grandparents, friends, and relatives had shared with us. At any extended pause, eight-year-old Fernando shouted out, "Tell another! Tell another!"

Share the Wonder: My niece Laura Ellen had mailed me a picture of Aaron when he was about two years old. When I next saw her, I asked her what had motivated her to send me that picture. "I just felt like I *should*," she said.

Then she whispered, "I have never told this to anyone, but while I was addressing your envelope, I kept making mistakes. I kind of felt Aaron's presence – then I kind of felt and heard him laughing – so much so that I burst out laughing myself."

Laura was collaborating with the dead, but didn't know it. Not yet. Shortly *after sharing her experience*, Aaron visited Laura in a dream. From her email:

> Hi Cathy. I had an incredible dream last night and just wanted to share. I don't know the exact details. I know that you, me, Kim, Ellen and Christy were doing some traveling. You took me to a cool little lake that always had a thin layer of ice covering the surface. It was strong enough to stand on, but you were able to see through the surface.

> In the dream, if you were able to find a pearl, then you would be blessed and rich. On the walk to this lake, you [Cathy] had asked Aaron, "to give Laura a sign that you are with us." I found a clam and, sure enough, a large pearl was inside of it.

Then we were sitting around a table. A clock struck 12, and I looked up and sitting right next to you was Aaron. He was beautiful. He was about 12 years old. Lips were red; skin so smooth and clear; hair blonde and a little spiky. He was the picture of health.

I started crying and said, "Oh, Aaron." I stood up to embrace him and he stood, wrapped his arms around me, and kissed my left temple. As I was hugging him, you must have known that I could see him. You were smiling and acting like you had expected this. Ellen was at the table too. The whole time I could hear a clock dinging in the background.

I woke up and felt very emotional … still feel it as I type this. Cool dream. It was so real. Just wanted to share.

Less than an hour after emailing me her dream, Laura's five-year-old daughter came home from shopping with her grandma, wearing a necklace of fantasy pearls that she had chosen – out of hundreds of options. **Click. Laura felt it.**

Laura now invites *all* family members to celebrate Christmas and she designs special decorations for those celebrating without a physical body.

Not long ago, she invited her cousin Diana, whose 1995 walk into death so shattered the lives of her family that they dare not speak of it – although Diana has tried. Appearing in the dreams of five broken hearts on the same night, in the same body, and in the same clothes, Diana spoke the same words to all.

Laura, Diana's sister Vicki, and perhaps many more, remain alert for Diana's invitations to collaborate on the furthering of the evolution of consciousness.

Their opening-door events are being documented and they are being shared.

Share Understanding: I wanted to thank my friend Chris for his loving kindness when Aaron left so abruptly, so I asked him to meet me for lunch. Or, at least that's why I thought I invited him. The idea to take the Directory and a Walk-About Book kept pushing its way into my mind, and, although I tried to talk myself out of it, I finally took them both.

When we met, Chris told me that as our phone call ended, he received a call from the Alzheimer facility caring for his mother, Eva, telling him to gather the family to say their goodbyes to her. My reluctance to share dissolved.

Chris knew that relationships continue past death and he shared his understanding with his family by creating a beautiful ceremony for them all: each one claimed a symbol to represent a special memory shared with Eva and each one entered her room individually. But *not* to tell her goodbye forever. They went to share their chosen symbol and to ask Eva to use it to communicate with them, after she died.

Desperate final farewells were modeled up into an occasion of mystery and wonder for *all* (including, dare we think, Eva herself?) and Chris thanked me repeatedly for having shared the opening-door events.

A few months later, I contacted Chris to ask if he had heard anything from his mom:

> Yes! Oh my God, Cathy! I have! One day I was kind of dozing in a chair, thinking and thinking about my mom and I *heard* her voice,[i] Cathy! She said, "I am so glad to be out of that damn residence!" Oh my God! Cathy, I was wide-awake and perfectly sober, and I *heard* her voice!

"Did you tell your kids?" I asked him. "Of course I did," he replied. Of course, indeed.

---

[i] As you now realize, Chris was in the hypnagogic state of consciousness.

Share a Family Directory: Opening a Family Directory opens the closed door of belief for the entire family. It doesn't matter that considerable time may pass before others cross the portal, because that is what time is for.

– **Carina and her sister Lili:** Inspired by Aniceto's 222, Carina began to document the frequent appearance of the numbers 11:11. After a few months, she **claimed** 11 as Lili's number and 11:11[i] as symbolic of a special collaboration between the two of them.

When she sent me documentation, I first put the information into *Finding Aaron* as a footnote. **CLICK.** I took of picture of my computer screen, shown below, and sent it to Carina.

with each other" have been made.
number 11.[11] It is absolutely true.

Carina shared this with her family in Argentina, instantaneously creating "Lili's group." Opening-door events now fly over continents, generating a field of receptivity for more events that are being documented and shared.

– **Cousin John Pepper:** An intuition to include a picture of Directory pages March 28 and 29 hounded me. I thought it was because my friend Rodrigo and my brother Eric share a March 28 birthday and the facing page hosts my cousin John and Chris' mom, Eva.

The idea occurred to me at the time that John might have had something to do with the intuition, but, finally, I talked myself out of it and deleted the picture.

---

[i] Claiming a number as a symbol is not about a number having a meaning to be deciphered. It is about the claimed number's mysterious medium of arrival. "The medium *is* the message" was said many years ago. *Collaboration with the dead* **is** the message.

Months later, the idea to include a picture of directory page February 13 came, VERY STRONGLY, to my mind.

This time, I thought it was because it seemed extraordinarily curious that Larry and Joaquin (the first two people that were consciously[i] entered into the Directory) share that birth date.

Complying with the intuition, I could only be still as the **CLICK flowed through my whole body**.

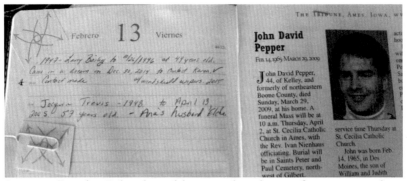

It *was* Cousin John knocking at the door of my everyday consciousness, asking me to please extend my vision and enlarge my understanding of the nature of things.[ii]

---

[i] That much of the collaboration with the dead is done unconsciously should surprise no one, as most of what we humans do is done unconsciously, until it becomes conscious. Making what is unconscious, conscious, is said to be the most human of human tasks and the purpose of life. That the most celebrated crusader of this vision, Carl Jung himself, consciously collaborated with the dead on the Great and Holy Work of furthering the evolution of consciousness is addressed very soon. Meanwhile, suffice it to say that, although it may not be well known, many of our heroes, saints, sages, and seers consciously worked with the dead.

[ii] Please notice that Larry left his physical body on an October 26 eighteen years prior to the October 26 of Claudelle's Celebration. Notice also that Claudelle's symbol is fixed to his entry. This is because Karen has recognized her dad's invitations to become aware of his collaboration. Joaquin's sticker is paper-clipped rather than fixed. This is because, as far as I know, his invitations are yet to be woven into his Family Tapestry.

– Cousin Conn Pepper: I was being fiercely bothered by the notion that I had to include a certain picture of Sister Luke walking for peace. I couldn't find that picture, but I couldn't stop looking for it. I even wrote to the Franciscan Canticle in Iowa to try to get a copy. I finally found it, folded and stapled to a page of the Directory that Sister Luke shares with my cousin, Conn. **CLICK. I knew it was Conn.**

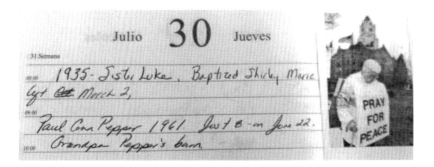

It is Conn's sister and my cousin Patty who gave me the beautiful expression, "That was orchestrated!" And so, it would seem, is all of this.

Share the Journey: I talked to Aaron's Grandma JoAnn Schaffer about communication from Aaron, day in and day out. Continuously. Tearfully. Breathlessly. Confusedly. JoAnn didn't bat an eye, having had numerous experiences herself.[i] It surprised me when I learned much later that she had not shared her experiences, at least not with her son, and Aaron's dad, Joe.[ii]

Joe was one of the very few people actually grateful for my rather incessant efforts at sharing the ever-accumulating evidence of collaboration with the dead. After his mind-changing experience of "HI DADDY" from the little boy with

---

[i] See page 167.
[ii] I venture to guess that JoAnn did share her experiences with Joe, but, at that time, he dismissed messages from long-dead relatives, phone calls from the dead, and visits with dead family members as nonsense.

the 1972 cap, Joe had made the commitment to document and share opening-door events – at least with his kids. Below is a bit of one of Joe's events that he also shared with me:

> So with the transmission out of the truck, we were stuck on the side of the highway. This is when the story gets interesting. A young man with a truck pulled up behind the trailer. When he got out of his truck and started walking toward me, I had to do a double take, as he looked so much like Aaron.
>
> He pulls trailers from the manufacturers to dealers throughout the country for a living, and he said he would pull our trailer to the campground. He pulled us to the campsite and helped me set up. [Joe's wife] Sheilah asked if he would stay and eat with us but he said he had to go as he was trying to get home for the Fourth of July.
>
> I tried to pay him and he pushed my hand away and told me just to pass it forward. I then felt the need to tell him about Aaron, and how much he resembled him. His response was, *"Maybe your son sent me to you."* I started to get teary-eyed (as I am now) and hugged him.

Joe had so opened his mind to the mystery called death that he was able to be with his mother as she died and call it "one of the most beautiful experiences I have ever had." He thanked me for **not** bucking up quietly, and he thanked Aaron for being so persistent. Then, so very suddenly, Joe was so very sick with cancer.

I completely understood his words when he wrote me, "Thanks to Aaron, I *know* that there is more after this life. I only hope that my kids will not see me suffer and that our son and my parents will meet me when I go." I replied to what seemed a still far-off event, "Hope has nothing to do with it, Of course they will be there." Then, in an instant, Joey was gone.

From deep within *that pain,* Joe's brother John told me, "Joe got so confused towards the end that he thought he was talking to Mom." Of course, Joe was not the one confused; he *was talking to their mom.* He was clear on some other things, too, like when he wrote, "I have been thinking about Aaron's #72 and thinking that the most logical # for me is 9/29 – my birth month and day. I use it a lot in passwords and such."

– **Joie Ray:** Thirteen days after her dad's death, Joe's daughter Joie Ray wrote to me:

> I got a call this morning, but there was no one there. Then the phone went busy. The number was 501/904-8873,[i] and when I looked at the time, it was **9:29.** I decided to call back. It said the number you dialed is not answering. Please try later. I called again and this time it said the number you dialed is temporarily unavailable. I sent you the recording that says the time and the phone number. Does this mean anything? Love, Joie.

– **Danielle:** On *March 10,* 2018, I called another of Joe's daughters to let her know that I was thinking of her and her dad on the one-year anniversary of his death. Danielle was crying when she answered the phone, but now with sorrow. She'd just had an opening-door event.

Sorely missing her father, Danielle was plodding through her everyday housework. Moving the couch, she saw a piece of paper wadded up in the corner. She picked it up and threw it away. But then, for some reason, she fished it out of the trash.

She unfolded it, and saw the flyer she had designed for a benefit she had wanted to host to help Joe cover some of the costs of his medical treatment. The date for the benefit was *March 10, 2017* – exactly the date that Joe had died. Danielle had forgotten the date of the benefit, but, dare we think, that Joe had not, and he wanted her to know?

---

[i] 48 had been claimed as the Schaffer number seven years earlier.

Joie and Danielle stumbled over truth, and neither one picked herself up and hurried off as if nothing had happened. They both documented and they both shared. What they do now is up to them. While it is true that neither need do a thing, it is just as true that both could do everything – as is true for us all.

I now **claim** an opening-door event of Alejo's from August 8, 2010: Alejo dreamed or heard a voice say, "Whose ken are we talking about?" He asked me, "What is *ken*? Spelled K-E-N?"

English *ken* is a cousin to the German *erkennen*:

- *Erkennen*: a process of knowledge involving perception, recognition, and discernment.

- *Knowledge*: facts, information, and skills acquired by a person through experience or education.

Alejo's opening-door event specifically uses KEN. He even got the spelling. Ken combines the two modes of gaining knowledge, i.e., experience and study, and includes all (but one) of the necessary components to acquire truth: discernment, recognition, perception, experience, and study. It is only missing the *key ingredient of motivation*.

There is nothing like seeking your lost love in the heart of the eternal to sustain the arduous endeavor of going beyond your beliefs about death all the way to acquiring truth.

The dead are not lost. They are simply not found. They are not found because they are not sought. And they are not sought because of the belief that finding the dead is impossible, irrelevant, irreverent, or dangerous.

Belief is such a crying shame. It wastes our sorrow just as surely as it squanders what is possibly the best method for heeding the most famous directive of all: *Know Thyself.*

Directive 11: Know Thyself

*"I am the man who, with utmost daring, discovered
what was discovered before."*
–G. K. Chesterton

Judging from the emphasis given to **Know Thyself** in every wisdom tradition sacred to humanity, this directive would seem to be the goal of the Great and Holy Work of furthering the evolution of consciousness.

The Self we are to know, however, is not the many-faceted person[i] navigating the world of matter, but the Immortal Self.

You may already know that the history of religion is full of seekers who came to know their immortal Self by collaborating with the dead. But it might surprise you to learn that many outside of the realm of religion claim the same collaborative partners. Case in point: Carl Jung.

Far too exhaustive a subject to attempt anything but the very briefest of introductions, the fact that Carl Jung collaborated extensively with the dead and carefully documented his experiences for many years,[ii] is far too important a fact to leave out.

In the first chapter of James Hillman and Sonu Shamdasani's book, *Lament of the Dead: Psychology After Jung's Red Book,* we read Shamdasani's words:

---

[i] *Person* comes from Latin *persona:* the theatrical masks worn in ancient times to indicate the varied roles played by the same actor, i.e., mother, wife, aunt, co-worker, etc. Switch roles – switch masks.

[ii] Called *The Red Book or Liber Novus,* the posthumous publication of Jung's documented collaboration with the dead is, in good part, thanks to the relentless efforts of Sonu Shamdasani. Insisting that this work is at the center of Jung's life and work, he negotiated with Jung's descendents to release the work for publication. After thirteen years of extensive editorial work, *The Red Book*, with its comprehensive introduction by Shamdasani, three appendices, and over 1500 editorial notes, is available to the public.

The work is Jung's "Book of the Dead." His descent into the underworld, in which there's an attempt to find the way of relating to the dead. He comes to the realization that unless we come to terms with the dead we simply cannot live, and that our life is dependent on finding answers to their unanswered questions.[29]

Shamdasani continues:

It is the ancestors. It is the dead. This is no mere metaphor. This is no cipher for the unconscious or something like that. **When he [Jung] talks about the dead he means the dead** [emphasis added]. And they're present in images. They still live on.[30]

And Hillman ponders:

But what are we to do now? What are we to do with this extraordinary thing? Because it seems to me those eighteen volumes of his [Jung's] have to be reconsidered ... .[31]

Shamdasini replies:

I've sometimes thought that if a fire broke out what text would I take? This is the text of Jung that I would take. And I would leave the rest. You can reconstruct so much of what is essential in what is to come in the rest of his works from this text.[32]

Let that sink in: Jung's *key work*, on which his theories and methods are based, *is clearly a collaboration with the dead*. Now, let this sink in: Jung's work is EVERYWHERE.

Psychiatry, psychology, history, anthropology, literature, alchemy, physics, astrology, astronomy, mathematics, philosophy, religious studies – you name any area of study or any facet of living, and, if looked for, Carl Jung's influence will be found. This means that every nook and cranny of our everyday walk about world is permeated with the collaboration of the dead.

One can well imagine Jung's difficulty in communicating his experiences with the dead, immersed as most of his readers were in the theory of material realism. This makes the fact that Jung chose not to publish *The Red Book* during his lifetime very understandable.

The theory of material realism is still confused with fact. I was advised, repeatedly, to "stop talking about collaborating with Aaron and *be rational.*" The speakers (unconsciously) meant that I should adhere to their belief in material realism, which forbids the possibility of collaborating with the dead.

Rational thought, however, is far more interesting than a simple endorsement of a worn-out metaphor. It is *a mode of experiencing* that transforms the immense electrical pulsation surrounding us into a never-ending series of separated "units" and "events."

Thanks to rational thought, humans experience a seemingly separate self that *can* be known. *But evolution of consciousness does not stop at rational thought.*

A fundamental premise of essential science and true spirituality is that humans are on the verge of modeling-up[i] from the "mental-rational structure"[ii] that gave rise to rational thought, to *"*an integral consciousness structure."

As its name implies, this new structure will *integrate,* and the theory is that what it will integrate are all the modes of experiencing that have unfolded through time, with the result that the modes will work together, synergistically.

---

[i] If Jung had published *The Red Book* before its time, pathologies to knowing and learning would have, no doubt, created a barrier of belief so thick that Jung's important work would not have been considered worth reading, and humanity would, most likely, not be quite so "on the verge."

[ii] The latest innovation of consciousness *to reach the masses.* See both Schafer's and Lachman's discussion of Jean Gebser's work.

When this restructuring of human consciousness becomes commonplace, it is predicted that the spiritual will be *concretized* and humanity will experience reality as the sages and saints have always done, so far ahead of the masses.

> As the word "concrete" suggests, this is a condition in which "the spiritual" becomes actually present and *perceivable*, no longer merely intuited, conceptualized, or felt.[33]

Phrases like "concretizing the spiritual" and "modes of experiencing consciousness through an integral consciousness structure" may sound strange and meaningless now.

But there is nothing so strange as how the strange becomes commonplace, and there is nothing so surprising as to discover that *seeking to understand collaboration with the physically dead gets you well on the way to this next consciousness structure*:

> When you become aware of the common roots of disconnected phenomena and principles, you have advanced to an important level of integrative thinking. From there you can proceed to yet higher levels, at which you allow the integrative mode of thinking to **restructure your consciousness** [my emphasis].

Essential science and true spirituality are now holding hands in their human quest for meaning and they are both telling us that the key to understanding the nature of reality is to *repent*.

Greek *metanoia* is translated as *repent*, but it never meant to ask for forgiveness of sins.[i] It meant to change your mind. Not to be confused with changing beliefs and opinions about things, *repent* is a call get up off your knees and join the Great and Holy Work of **changing the structure of the mind itself,** i.e., to engage in the furthering of the evolution of consciousness.

---

[i] Greek *hamartia,* translated as *sin*, is an archery term for "miss the mark."

I now **claim** an opening-door event of November 8, 2010: I woke up remembering that a priest kept asking me, insisting that I find out, "What is the first thing that Jesus says in the Bible?" I *recognized* the answer five years later in Marvin Meyer's translation of the Gospel of Thomas:[i]

These are the hidden sayings that the living Yeshua spoke and
Yehuda Toma the twin recorded.
And he said,
Whoever discovers what these sayings mean will not taste death.
Yeshua said,
Seek and do not stop seeking until you find.
When you find, you will be troubled.
When you are troubled, you will marvel
and rule over all.[34]

The Gospel of Thomas is the oldest gospel found so far, making "the first thing that Jesus says in the Bible" no less than: *seek the truth about death until you find it.* And the recommended method is certainly **not** to believe. It is *to marvel.*

Marvel did not mean to sit in a stupor of amazement. It meant to contemplate, to study, to search and research. It meant to acquire truth – about death. This is what we are all born to do.

---

[i] In the year 325 C. E., Emperor Constantine convened a group of clerics to select "appropriate texts" for what would be called The New Testament. During the intense struggle to define Christian orthodoxy, more than fifty texts were excluded and became outlawed. Fearing their destruction, "heretics" buried them near the Upper Egyptian town of Nag Hammadi, where they remained until 1945. The Gospel of Thomas is one of them. This is a compilation of sayings attributed to Jesus, recorded by his closest associates while they were working with him. *They show a knowing about death.* Why was The Gospel of Thomas not included in The New Testament? Many reasons have been suggested, but I wonder if the selection committee simply could not (that is, they were *unable to*) believe what they were reading and *would not seek to understand*, not beyond their beliefs anyway. Read the Nag Hammadi Library. Decide for yourself what Jesus and his associates *knew*, and were trying to share.

Perhaps it is not so much that we are "born here" to balance our karma, learn this lesson, or do that deed, but we are "born here" because we have not yet experienced our immortality.

Perhaps this is a place whose purpose is to be a home where those who claim they *do not know themselves* can come to question what they are, as *A Course in Miracles* proposes.

Perhaps there is a coming and going – in and out, and in and out – of material form in the world of matter, that goes on and on, until we heed our trumpet call, and finally *experience* our own immortality.

The Benedictine monk's understanding of the message of Jesus would then make perfect sense. To become aware of the presence of the dead to develop a vital relationship with them would be to come to know our immortal Self.

The instructions at Peter Marshall's funeral to endeavor to know Peter in spirit just as he had been known in the flesh are to further the Great and Holy Work of evolving consciousness.

Pastor Stacey's words ring true: The world is one spirit and the dead do invite us to collaborate with them to further the evolution of consciousness.

The man who came to my school gave the most powerful recruiting speech of all: by learning to see "with Christ's vision that no one is a body," we come to *know* our Aarons in spirit. And, thus it is, that we come to know, once and for all, what we are, and what we are not.

We are not a plague or a virus, nor are we aliens stranded on a cold, lifeless rock. We are not a result of mindless matter accidently bumping itself into shape, nor are we pots spun off a wheel, breathed into life by a master potter, and placed here to wait for a death that will set us free.

We are an emanation out of that Life Force called God by some, but known world-wide by many different names. A Life Force that did not so much create the universe as it *became* the universe, *is* the universe.

We are all fruit of the same womb, acorns of the same tree, and seeds of the same vine. And, as Alan Watts is surely still so fond of saying, "as apple trees apple, this universe peoples."

We are beings of consciousness blossoming out as matter, forever alive and always living in a spiritual world, doing our best to further the evolution of what we are.

Know Thyself

Therefore man must obtain self-knowledge or spiritual knowledge by raising his level. (Vedas 1700 – 1100 BCE).

Enquiry into the truth of the Self is knowledge. (Upanishads, circa 650 BCE).

Knowing others is intelligence, knowing yourself is true wisdom. (The Tao Te Ching, circa 400 BCE).

Yeshua said: When you know yourselves, then you will be known, and you will understand that you are children of the living father. Whoever finds himself is superior to the world. (Gospel of Thomas, 40 CE).

And do thou, O Muhammad, remember thy Lord within thyself. (The Koran, 632 CE).

He who knows himself knows God. (Al-Ghazzali, 1058 – 1111).

I searched for God and found only myself. I searched for myself and found only God. (Rumi, 1207 – 1273).

The eye through which I see God is the same eye through which God sees me; my eye and God's eye are one eye, one seeing, one knowing, one love. (Meister Eckhart, 1260 – 1328).

My Me is God, nor do I recognize any other Me except my God Himself. (St. Catherine of Genoa, 1447 – 1510).

The highest aim of religion is Self-knowledge. (Sri Yukteswar Giri, 1855 – 1936).

At the center of the universe dwells the Great Spirit. And that center is really everywhere. It is within each of us. (Black Elk, 1863 – 1950).

Jesus Christ knew he was God. So wake up and find out eventually who you really are. In our culture, of course, they'll say you're crazy and you're blasphemous, and they'll either put you in jail or in a nut house (which is pretty much the same thing). However if you wake up in India and tell your friends and relations, 'My goodness, I've just discovered that I'm God,' they'll laugh and say, 'Oh, congratulations, at last you found out.'" (Alan Watts, 1915 – 1973).

With this we have reached a defining point of our humanity whose implications are giant. If the inner images in us are cosmic, it could mean that we are connected with the cosmic potentiality. It could mean that we are part of a cosmic field that is acting in us. Of course, spiritual teachers of all times have told us all along that something like this is going on: God is in you. But to discover hints of a cosmic presence and cosmic activities within us, in the context of science's description of the world, redefines the playing field. It allows us to consider the matter without archaic threats and darkness. (Lothar Schafer, 1939 –).

It is the joy of knowing yourself as the very life essence before life takes on form. That is the joy of being – of being who you truly are (Eckhart Tolle, 1945 –).

Epilogue

"Share the Joy." –Aniceto Sánchez Medina

I was told repeatedly that "getting through Aaron's death" would be the hardest work I would ever do. This is true.

I was also told repeatedly that I had to either settle for a belief that Aaron was still living, or buck up and bear *that pain* of accepting that he was gone. This is not true. No matter how many times it is repeated.

My first invitations (the first that I recognized anyway) to learn a mode of experiencing the range of human spiritual life where the dead live, were from my father-in-law, Aniceto.

Communication from Aniceto after his death was so constant that no one could deny it.

One day Alejo asked his dad, "But Viejo, what do I DO with all this?" Aniceto's answer was to **SHARE THE JOY.**

Finding Aaron did not feel complete without including Aniceto's directive, but Joy was then still a place that I could only glimpse from afar. On July 18, 2016, the idea came to me to add his directive as an Epilogue.

```
COPI  CARRUS
  CARMEN MUÑOZ PEREZ
   CIF. 33.479.943 - Q
C/ JOSE BERNAD AMOROS 38
     03205  ELCHE

00#0045        18/07/2016
13:26   EMP A

74X                   @0,03
FOTOCO B/N             2,22
SUB TOTAL             2,22

CAJA                  2,22

     IVA INCLUIDO
```

With my heart pounding, and full of emotion, I made copies of that version of *Finding Aaron*. The cost was **2.22** Euros. **Aniceto's number. CLICK. I felt it. It felt like joy.**

Going beyond one's beliefs to acquire any deep truth is hard work, but I can vouch for something that I think I read somewhere: "To recognize a subtle communication from the dead comes with a mystical sense of meaning so intense that it makes all effort at understanding worthwhile."

It is this effort at understanding that clarifies the unconditional meaningfulness of life: consciousness doesn't end – it evolves.

Those who confuse the theory of material realism with truth won't make the effort to find this out for themselves because they are (unconsciously) convinced that what they want to find cannot be found. Thus, belief is better than nothing.

This is the genesis of today's infatuation with **BELIEVE**. Seen everywhere, from church billboards to coffee cups and T-shirts, **BELIEVE** is promoted as the solution. But belief is not a solution to anything; it is the problem. The solution is to acquire truth. And everyone *can*.

I hope that *Finding Aaron* inspires you to **acquire truth about death for yourself.**

Seek your lost loves beyond where you believe them to be. The love that fills your broken heart will sustain you as it sustains all who acquire the truth about death.[i]

Remain ever receptive to wonder and alert to synchronicities. Document your experiences as you search and research. Continuously model-up your understanding of truth as there is no final model of any final truth possible, because seeking evolves the seeker (consciousness) as well as what is being sought (consciousness). And seeking the truth about death is what we are all born to do.

---

[i] There has never been a safer place nor a better time to acquire the truth about the mysteries of birth, death, the Power that we call God, and the I that we call Self, than in the West *right now*. All through the ages many in the West were executed, as was Socrates, for the impious acts of refusing to declare allegiance to the Gods recognized by the community and for introducing new metaphors/models for God. But not any more.

As *Finding Aaron* comes to a close on September 17, 2018, Alejo shares a dream:

> "I had a dream with Aaron this morning. You remember the dream with my dad where I became conscious I was dreaming and not wanting to miss my chance to be nice to him?"
> "Yes, I remember," I said.
> "This was the same, but between me and Aaron. I was writing a sort of memoir, which I had titled, *My True Story*. I was working on it when Aaron came from behind; read the title, smiled, patted me gently on the head and kissed me. Then he left."

Everyone's true story is, of course, the one and same story of daring to discover **for yourself,** what was discovered before.

Do the dishes, drive the kids, fix the roof, go to meetings, but
through it all remain aware that we are spiritual beings,
immersed in a spiritual experience *labeled* human.
Remember that the heaven which is spread upon
the earth is beyond the KEN only of those
who won't know. Document the gold that
does not glitter, because notation
facilitates the discovery
that matter is spirit
and spirit
matters,
as you and as me and as everything else.
Right here and right *now*. Forever and Ever, Amen.

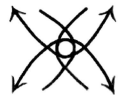

Appendix

The knowledge, that in human nature there is an eternal core of being
which passes through birth and death-this knowledge, remote as it is to
the modern mind, is comparatively easy to attain, and it will certainly
be attained by those who have enough perseverance.

–Rudolf Steiner

Leibniz is right – notation does facilitate discovery. It does so
by developing integrative thinking.

What follows are the entries for the full year of July 2, 2010
through July 2, 2011, edited for better reading. Entries that end
with an ellipsis […] are already mentioned in the text of
Finding Aaron.

This appendix is included to demonstrate the importance of
noting EVERYTHING that feels connected to your dead right
away. Don't wait. Not only will you forget, but your
pathologies of knowing and learning will be hard at work
defending your unconscious beliefs by trying to convince you
that what you experienced is meaningless.

July 5: (When they were together, Aaron and his Aunt Kim
always went out for morning coffee. Aaron made fun of Kim
for spending so much on fancy coffee while he paid 25 cents
for his cup of plain black coffee.)

Today Kim got her coffee at the Starbucks where she and
Aaron went. (He bought his coffee at QuikTrip.) She has gone
here hundreds of time. They know her. Kim doesn't even order
her peppermint latte; they see her and get it ready. This time,
the correct order was written on her cup, but it was plain black
coffee. Kim said she felt Aaron's presence and told him to quit
giving her crap.

July 8: At 2:30 in the morning, I had a dream that was not
really a dream but was more like words that I somehow *felt …*

(The thing is – I FELT the joy and peace. And I didn't hear the words, but I FELT them. It's like they were being impressed upon my mind. They came out of my mouth onto the recorder, but they were not from my own mind. I was being told the information. I *knew* it. There was no question about what was being said.)

July 13: The cab taking us to Aaron's service in Barcelona had registration number 2772 …

July 14 – pendulum: Aaron's friend Mariangel called me and said that she has "worked the pendulum for seven years" (whatever that means) and that she was in contact with Aaron. She said that Aaron wanted her to tell me that:

> He was always hassling you about your belief that most people are good. He says he did that for your protection. He understands more now. He says, "Thank you a thousand times for all the love. You are so generous with your love. To please be careful with your health."

This seemed so general as to be meaningless. Thinking of the experience of July 8, I asked her to check if he had sent a message last Thursday, and, if so, what was the message? The answer was, in fact, the July 8 message:

> Yes, it was me. The message was "to be patient with yourself. That patience is your virtue. To please be as patient with yourself as you were with me."

July 16: Christy and I walked to the little chapel …

July 24 – Des Moines: Aaron's funeral. I faint and go. A woman appeared out of nowhere with a stack of books …

July 29: Kandy wants to make a scrapbook of her and Aaron's travels. The store was out. Kandy lifts up a piece of paper with AARON written on it to find the one scrapbook in the store.

August 2: Aaron's car started spontaneously today …

August 3: In the middle of the night, LOUD symphony music woke [my sister] Ellen. She got out of bed and went outside to see if it was her neighbors. NO. She was now wide-awake. Still she heard the music. Today is her birthday.

August 4: Waking up, I saw a newspaper with the word SON and a picture of the sun shining. "72 degrees" was in the upper right-hand corner in BIG letters. It was not exactly a dream, but more like a vision. (Now I know it was the state of consciousness called hypnogogia.)

August 4: Longtime friend Irene called me to say that she never remembers dreams, but she remembered this one and felt that she should call me. She was going for a ride. It was raining. The car windows were down and the front seat was full of mud; written in the mud, as if with a finger, was, "Tell Cathy to be strong."

August 7: On Kandy's flight back to Spain, the airplane …

August 8: *Waking up,* Alejo dreams or hears the words, "Whose ken are we talking about …"

Later, we bought two books.[i] When we sat down to look through them, Alejo felt a vibration – like a cell phone – in his shirt pocket. Three times. He had no cell phone.

August 10: Almost awake, I saw AARON'S FACE and a pink Mother's Day card. Written in his handwriting at about age six, were the words: SAME MOMMY. SAME THINK. It felt so important that I wrote the words in the dark. (Hypnogogia.)

---

[i] The books turn out to be CLASSICS in the field of Afterlife Science: *Life Beyond Death* by Arthur Ford and *Life After Life* by Raymond Moody. Moody made a *highly recommended* documentary by the same name.

August 12: Alejo and I went to see Rob, my high school friend who is now a lawyer, about something. I don't remember what. All I could do was weep. Rob told me to stop thinking of killing myself. "The time here is a grain of sand on a beach," he said. "There is much more to life than this life."

Rob told us that when his grandmother died he was only nineteen years old. He got to the house late, and he went immediately into her bedroom.

Her body stayed in the bed, he said, but her spirit left that body and talked with him. She told him not to cry. That she has a wonderful family and had had a wonderful life with them. Later, when he and his cousins were talking about their grandmother, a roll-up door on her china cupboard opened.

Rob took his sister's obituary out of his desk drawer. She was only 35 years old – she taught English in Japan and China, and was a professor at Berkeley. She came to Des Moines to visit, and was killed in an automobile accident at 63rd and Grand.

(At this time, I had no way of understanding Rob's experience. I knew that he wasn't lying, but I struggled with "How can this possibly be true?")

August 17: In the middle of the night, the words "change the Y to I, and add ED" were pounding so fiercely into my head that I had to write them down. It seems more like, "Change the *why* to I, and add ED." What is this? Seems connected to the "same mommy, same think" vision-like thing. (Hypnagogia.)

August 18: We took Aaron's car for a maintenance check. We were the first to arrive and went into the office. We were told to go into the service area. We were still the only customers.

Pulling into the service area, a woman arrived and Alejo motioned her to go first.

The bill shows 73 as our customer number, but our real number is 72. Aaron's number for sure is 72.

Bill from the Land Rover Dealership.

August 19: Ellen had a sort of vision. It felt important. We were sitting on a couch and a bright, bright, BRIGHT light came to the window and shattered it. The noise of the shattering glass woke her up completely.

August 20: Falling asleep, I could feel Aaron's presence, but it seemed like I was blocking him, or something.

August 22: Many, many nights, my forlorn wailing would fill the forest surrounding Christy's cabin. This night Christy whispered, "Listen. The coyotes are ANSWERING you." A strangely mystical peace descended for a few minutes. It was awe-inspiring. I could almost hear the wind speaking.

August 24: Alejo saw a bolt on a path. For some reason, he picked it up and put it in his pocket. Aaron's car overheated. When it cooled down, Alejo saw nothing but, feeling around, he did feel a loose clamp that was missing a bolt. The thought came to him, "Maybe this is why I took the bolt. Maybe it is a message." Alejo got the bolt and it fit perfectly.

August 27: In Spain, Kandy needed to call a co-worker, but was out of cell-phone range. She stopped at a rest area with public telephones but could not understand the instructions. For some reason, a man came over and asked if she needed help. He was not a native speaker of Spanish, and had a strong accent. She thanked him and asked, "What is your name?"

"Aaron," he answered. Kandy said that she was so shocked that she asked him his name three times. (*Aaron* is not a name commonly heard in Spain. This is only the second Aaron Kandy has ever met.)

September 1: People are giving out coffee at a rest area in Idaho. I went to a booth and started crying that my son had died. The woman hugged me, saying, "My son died 20 years ago. He was such a wonderful son. He always called and got recipes and told me how great I looked. Not a day goes by that I don't think of him and talk to him. Oh, how my heart goes out to you. I cried for SUCH a long time." Why did I go to *her* stand?

September 2: Kandy looked all over Barcelona for the movie *City of Angels*. She told the wonderful man, who had registered her and Aaron in the video club, what she was looking for. He told her, "Kandy, please don't watch that movie. It is too sad." She couldn't find it, but she couldn't stop looking for it.

Today, at 2:30 in the morning, Kandy "decided to get up and watch television." (This is VERY unlike her – Kandy doesn't watch television, let alone at 2:30 in the morning.) She turned on the television. *City of Angels* was *starting*.

September 13: Doing laundry, I couldn't find two of Aaron's socks. I got panicky. Ellen and Alejo joined the search. We moved the dryer, checked everywhere. Then Ellen said, "Okay, Baron, [Aaron's nickname with the Jensens] this isn't funny anymore. Your mom feels bad," and walked straight to the couch where we all had looked before – there were both socks. Plain as day. Ellen said she could almost feel Aaron laughing.

September 27: Researching the possibility of seeing a medium on Aaron's birthday, I came across an activity called *A Necessary Journey.* I liked the title; it was on Aaron's birthday and was close to Christy's, where I planned to be, so I decided to buy tickets with "Aaron's Relia Card."* Then the idea came to me to get the balance on the card. **$22.72.**

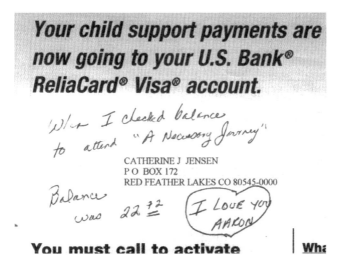

Your child support payments are now going to your U.S. Bank® ReliaCard® Visa® account.

When I checked balances to attend "A Necessary Journey"

CATHERINE J JENSEN
P O BOX 172
RED FEATHER LAKES CO 80545-0000

Balance was 22.72

I LOVE YOU AARON

You must call to activate

Wh

*When Aaron was about thirty years old, the state of Iowa recovered back child support from his dad, Joe Schaffer. Aaron and I always laughed about the late collection and I only used what I called "Aaron's card" when the two of us were together.

September 28: Kandy was getting ready to drive to a job sight when a friend she had not talked to for years called her about Aaron. Then it was very late. Being a new driver, Kandy was nervous about driving in the mountains in the dark. She asked Aaron to help her and left. When Kandy arrived at her hotel, the woman told her, "Thank God you didn't come earlier. A storm blew through here like a cyclone, with extremely high winds."

October 1: Aaron's sister, Joie Ray, was doing Facebook. She got up to get a cup of coffee. When she returned, Aaron's picture was on her computer screen. She says that to get the picture she would have had to have been on his profile and then clicked it.

October 2: Kim showed up as a witness at the Land Rover …

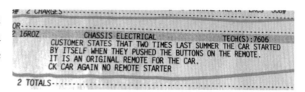

2 CHARGES

OR
2 16ROZ   CHASSIS ELECTRICAL   TECH(S):7606
CUSTOMER STATES THAT TWO TIMES LAST SUMMER THE CAR STARTED
BY ITSELF WHEN THEY PUSHED THE BUTTONS ON THE REMOTE.
IT IS AN ORIGINAL REMOTE FOR THE CAR.
CK CAR AGAIN NO REMOTE STARTER

2 TOTALS

October 3: Because of Aaron's interest in crystals, I bought a book on the subject. I learned that the stone on the necklace that he made me is *amethyst*. It was in the headdress of the high priest *Aaron,* brother of Moses. The book says that amethyst is used to help with trauma and grief; that it helps open the seventh chakra to *receive information from spirits*. It is the crystal for Aquarius, [i] "my sign." Did Aaron know these things?

October 4: As I pulled out of JoAnn's driveway with Aaron's things in the back seat, a car almost hit me – license plate 222. I was going to have a salad but then changed my mind and had sushi. [In honor of having had eaten it for the first time with Aaron in Spain.] The price code on the container was 7222.

I picked up Aaron's 10-year-old nephew, Josiah. He told me that he had invited Aaron to be his friend on Facebook.

---

[i] Psychologist Rosa Elena recommended that I have a natal chart prepared by an astrologer. I *believed* it was utter nonsense, but I went anyway. The result was a *powerful* opening-door event. Concerning astrology, I recommend Ray Grasse's book, *The Waking Dream: Unlocking the Symbolic Language of Our Lives.*

"Before he died?" I asked. "No," Josiah answered. "After, in case his spirit wants to."

October 6: A woman mistakenly called Kim repeatedly. Today Kim asked her, "What number are you trying to call?" XXX-XX**72**. Kim asked, "Who do you want to talk to?" The woman answered, "*Christy*."

October 10: Alejo's dream: Alejo saw Aaron seated on a couch, bent over with his arms on his legs, thumbing through a magazine. Alejo told him, "Aaron, you can't be here. You are dead." Aaron doesn't acknowledge him. Alejo decides to ignore him, thinking, "I must be having a vision," and goes upstairs to a bathroom with many shower stalls. Alejo takes a quick shower and because the glass was translucent, he sees someone in the next stall and asks:

"Aaron, is that you?"
"Yes."
"You look okay. Are you okay?"
"Yes."
"Shall I tell your mom that you are okay?"
"Yes, tell my mom I'm okay."

October 17: Laura's tree planting ceremony for Aaron. Brad tells me that his connection with Aaron is all about football …

October 19: Driving to Lafayette, Indiana, I camped at Lake Ahquabi. The park ranger brought me the registration …

October 21: Went with Tom to see the football bus …

October 22: Go to the bank … . Go to meet Dave the lawyer, but no one was in the office …

October 23: Driving from Lafayette to Christy's, I pass through Keokuk, Iowa. I decide to stay here because of a trip

Aaron and I took when he was five, to become better acquainted with Chief Keokuk. A local hotel calls my attention, but I think "no," and drive by. Then "I decide" to turn around and go back.

The office was full of pictures of Jesus, prompting me to burst into tears and tell the stranger behind the desk, "My son Aaron died. He died. I can't do this. I want to die."

Philip came out from behind the counter and hugged me. "I know how you are feeling," he said. "My wife's daughter **Erin** died many years ago. I find her crying and I know why." He asked me if I had grandchildren. "No, Aaron and my daughter-in-law, **Kandy**, were starting to talk about adopting."

Asked Phillip Thayer to pray for me – Lobby was full of pictures of Jesus. I cried. He hugged me so beautifully and told me – I understand. My wife's daughter Erin died at 13. Many years ago. When I see her crying, I know why. Chatting – he said "My daughter in law Candy ...."

"That's curious," Philip told me. "My daughter-in-law's name is also **Candy**. My son just told me that they are thinking to adopt children. Very curious, don't you think? The names Erin and Candy – and I only just found out that they are thinking about adoption." **CLICK. We both felt it**.

October 24: I drive through Tecumseh, Nebraska, and, because Tecumseh is Aaron's favorite Indian hero, I decide to sleep here. I see a local hotel with picnic tables and grills, like a place you could rent while you were working cable (as Aaron did), and I decide to stay here.

The owner brings towels to my room. Seeing Aaron's picture and the lit candle, she asked me what happened – then she began to cry. She told me that her sister **Cathy's** son died a year ago, and that the entire family was staggering with grief. I tried to share what was happening with the messages, but it came out all garbled. It was comforting to say it though, and it did seem to comfort her too.

Tecumseh was a calming and seemingly very safe place. The owner told me that the church down the road was always unlocked and I could go there at any time during the night. I took a walk and leaned against a big oak tree until four in the morning. It was so strangely beautiful. It reminded me of the night the coyotes called to Alejo, Christy, and me.

October 30: Dad died one year ago today. Christy and I set up a double altar. We put out flowers and candles, and many personal items. Christy's house was for sale, and a couple knocked on the door, wanting to look through the house. I invited them in.

Seeing our altar, the man told me that his dad had died a short time ago. He had his dad's tattoos on his own arm. He asked me all about Dad and Aaron. He hugged me so sincerely. His birthday is the same as L. J. Schaffer's birthday, November 8. (Two years later, I would be told to be especially alert on November 8.)

November 1: I took Aaron's car to Casey's Car Wash for his birthday …

I called Alejo to tell him that Aaron's car had somehow moved itself and that Casey's Car Wash was going to replace Aaron's already damaged bumper. His mom answered. I did not have the strength to speak in Spanish, so I hung up. *And I felt really bad that I had.* About thirty seconds later, Christy's phone RANG and I answered it. Christy was a witness – the phone rang. It was Alejo's mom. I asked her how she called me. "I didn't call you," she said. "You called me." Alejo checked. There is no callback button on her phone.

November 2: Christy went with me to Casey's Car Wash …

Ellen came for Aaron's birthday. Her plane arrived at 2:22. Her flight was 2 hours and 22 minutes.

November 3: Aaron's birthday. Four of us went to *A Necessary Journey*, the story of Bingh Rybacki's response to the death of her baby Garth.

Bingh felt the need to go home to Vietnam, where she found 27 (Aaron's number with Kandy) orphans "waiting for her" in a monastery. The thought came to her, "Shall I simply forget *this pain* and continue in my normal life?" NO! Her answer was to found Children of Peace International (COPI). Her story felt very meaningful to me.

November 5: The book *Raymond* arrived …

November 8: I woke up remembering that a priest kept asking me "What is the first thing that Jesus says in the Bible?" and I *knew* that this was very important …

November 15: Kandy was reading a book and got up to do something. Then she couldn't find the book. She looked and looked.

Kandy remembered Ellen saying, "Okay Aaron – this isn't funny anymore" about the socks, and said aloud, "Aaron! That's enough!" The book fell to the floor with a loud bang.

November 17: Today was the first meeting of *JAGGED*: The *Jim and Aaron Grief Group, Emotionally Distressed*, created by Ellen and her friend Kathy, whose broken heart aches for her husband Jim.

November 18: One year ago today, Aaron headed to Spain. The top half of my body slowly became paralyzed …

November 24: Thanksgiving. I watched the movie, *"an unfinished life."* It feels realistic. Ten years after this guy's son died, he still feels angry and unmotivated to live. Deep despair is what I feel. I chopped off another big chunk of my hair.

November 26: Elcy, a neighbor in Venezuela, called me at Christy's. I was amazed, knowing how difficult it would have been for her to make the call.[i]

"I had to call you," she told me. "I had a dream with your son. He was lying on a bed with blue curtains surrounding him. The entire room was bathed in blue light. He told me, 'I know that you and my mom interact. You must tell my mom that I am okay.'"

November 28: Kim saw a family of blonde-headed kids at church. One of them reminded her very strongly of Aaron when he was about ten and spending a lot of time with her and Brad. She felt compelled to watch this little boy. When everyone stood up to sing, SCHAFFER (Aaron's last name) was on the back of this child's shirt.

December 2: Looking for books on after-death science, the title *To Live Again* catches my eye …

December 7: Coming into Mom's apartment, I ask her, "What time is *Jeopardy* on? Maybe we can catch the end of it." I turned on the television to hear the bonus question, "What is mentioned several times in the Bible and in John II?" Without thinking, "raising the dead" came out of my mouth.

---

[i] Elcy lives in rural Venezuela, with no phone and no easy transportation to get to one. She explained that she felt *compelled to call me.* When I returned to Venezuela, Elcy and her daughter Carolina (as a witness to her mom's experience) made a trip to my farm to tell me in person that when Elcy had the dream about Aaron, she didn't know that he had died. She found out two days later. They were both overwhelmed with emotion.

That was correct. I have no idea what it says anywhere in the Bible. **Why did I say that? Where did it come from?** No other day did I even think about *Jeopardy*.

December 8: Kandy called to say that she woke up repeating the words: "El trato fue no habría plan." This translates into, "The deal was, there would be no plan." (Hypnogogia.)

December 9: Brad and I were together when the number 53 jersey that Matt Kroel used while playing with the Hawkeyes arrived. The box had packing number **222. CLICK.** Brad gasped. At that moment in time, he *knew.* The immense fulfillment of sharing the mystery was beyond words. (See the reading with medium Angelina Diana.)

The box that the jersey came in.

December 13: I notice that my new CD by the Grateful Dead (Aaron's favorite band) is a recording of their **22**-country tour performed in **1972**. I read somewhere that the name for the band comes from a story about a dead person being grateful to a living person for helping him.

December 25: As she was coming down the stairs, the cold ashes in Ellen's wood stove BURST into flames. She said, "Merry Christmas, Barony."

December 28: I woke up repeating the words Ergium Sanctium …

December 30: I WON THE RAFFLE from the Forever Family Foundation!!!!!!

December 31: I prayed all night to die.

January 6: I woke up with "GET THE ALAN WATTS book" strong on my mind. (I had picked up this book years ago, but had never read it.) Asking for a message, I opened the book to see Aaron's favorite expression, *"Chop wood, carry water."*

This was my introduction to Alan Watts, who has become so instrumental in my quest. Typing this up on January 6, 2018, seven years after it happened, I get the intuition to look for Alan Watts' birthday. It is **TODAY, JANUARY 6**. Document with dates.

January 13: I got a feeling about the book *When Bad Things Happen to Good People*. I have never read it. Alejo found a recording of the author, and, listening to it, we heard, "My wife and I were struggling in our grief over our only child's death. **Aaron** was only four …"

January 21: Waking up, Alejo told me his dream. "I heard someone say, 'There is a disaster in Saint Lucia' [he pronounced it in English], and I said, 'Oh you mean Santa Lucia' [he pronounced it in Spanish]. That's an island in the Caribbean.'" Alejo then got up and turned on the radio and we both heard the announcer saying, "There was a disaster in the cathedral Santa Lucia in Maracaibo [Venezuela] during the night …"

January 22: Aniceto died nine years ago today. Alejo and I went to the cemetery. Crossing the road, a car with license plate 22I passes in front of me. Parked car was 2LP72.

On our way home, we stopped to get movies. A man about Aaron's age arrives, looks like a weight lifter [as Aaron was] and has on an INDIANA t-shirt. [Aaron lived in Indiana many years.] My legs buckled. I could not make myself understood in the store and just wept. Alejo came in to find me.

At home, we decide to watch the movie *About Schmidt.* In the movie, donations are solicited for an group that helps children. I hear: "for only **22** dollars a month, only **72** cents a day …"

January 27: Reading with medium Angelina Diana …

February 18: Alejo and I go to buy electronics. The car next to us was poorly parked, and we have to squeeze into the parking spot. I decide to wait by a nearby building, in case I need to move our car so the other driver can get into his.

I kept feeling stupid about waiting outside in the heat, and went back and forth in my mind about going into the air conditioning. I look up and see a billboard that says, in Spanish, JUNTOS [meaning together] and then in English, ABOVE. So, it says, *together above*, using both languages.

The owner of the other car finally returns, wearing a shirt with *Ecko Unltd 1972.* I felt myself growing light, like floating, as if I were leaving my body. I crouched to my knees and pressed into the side of the building to get steady.

March 1: My sister Ellen and her friend Mike were walking their dogs. A snowball hit Ellen's left shoulder, right below her shoulder blade. There was snow in the trees and she thought, "That's a weird angle; snow couldn't fall like that from the trees."

Without thinking she said, "AARON?" Then she said, "Aaron, if that's really you, do it again." Three seconds later another snowball hit her right side, under her shoulder blade. She called to Mike, "Are you throwing snowballs?" He was bewildered. No, he was not.

March 2: A phrase, which I wrote down as *"4 words on the walls of Balashar's palace,"* woke me up in the middle of the night. They were so bizarre, yet so strong on my mind that I had to write them down in the dark.

(I had made myself a rule that I could not actively research any of the words and phrases that were coming to me in what I later learned was hypnogogia. Instead, I had to "let the explanations come to me." This explanation took about two years.)

> *November 2, 2013.* I was at Christy's for Aaron's birthday. I looked through my books for something to read to fall sleep, and decided on *A Search for the Truth* by Ruth Montgomery. Glancing at the table of contents, I chose Chapter 20: "This Wonderful Psychic World," and opened to page **272**.
>
> On the facing page I read, "In the old testament we read of the materialized hand, which appeared at King Belshazzar's feast and wrote on the wall, "Mene, mene, tekel, upharsia." **Oh my God! The four words on Balashar's palace.**

(The spelling of Belshazzar is different from my phonetic spelling of *Balashar,* but this is the message I had received in hypnagogia last March.)

Calling this "writing on the wall" an example of automatic writing, Montgomery gives reasons why the Judeo-Christian religion is the logical realm for pursuing psychical study and sites Biblical scholar Alfred E. Turner's declaration that over 145 different types of psychic phenomena are encountered in the Bible.

"Paradoxically," she says, "it is the clergy who most often discount the possibility of spirit communication while simultaneously warning against making the attempt to communicate." Paradoxically, indeed.

THIS WONDERFUL PSYCHIC WORLD : 273

the mount with Christ. An angel appeared to the two Marys at the sepulcher, to the shepherds at the time of Christ's birth, to Peter in prison, and to Paul in a vision.

In the Old Testament we read of the materialized hand, which appeared at King Belshazzar's feast and wrote on the wall: "Mene, mene, tekel, upharsin"—an example of automatic writing. Joshua saw and conversed with a spirit who

oh my god I, I...

March 8: Bought tickets to Forever Family Foundation's Earth Day Raffle.

March 10: Kandy and I were driving Aaron's car from Colorado to Iowa when Kandy said, "Can we stop at that little gas station?"
"It's awful small. The bathrooms might not be clean," I began as I pulled in.
Out of the car, Kandy says, "Cathy, look at the name."

A.J.'s C-Store – A.J. is Aaron's nickname on the Schaffer side of his family. It was here that Kandy's two-month search for a travel coffee mug ended as she bought one that suited her: La Rue Coffee, 1972.

Two years later – same highway, same car, same destination – I began to wonder about that little gas station. I saw it, pulled in, and parked. Then, for some reason, I checked the odometer – 106.**272**. Teresa Brume, who

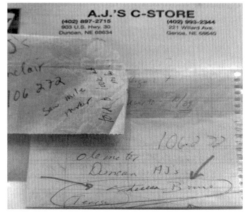

remembered selling us the travel mug two years earlier, verified the odometer reading and signed as a witness.

March 21: JoAnn Schaffer asked for some of the ashes of Aaron's physical body to be buried with her. She says she will have a plaque made that says *Beloved Grandson Aaron*.

When she, Mom, Kandy, and I went to see her burial plot, JoAnn shared many opening-door events: Her mother appeared to her twice after her death and she has seen her husband L.J. twice, so far. She told us, "When L.J. died, the phone rang, and I answered it. It was Monsignor Griswald telling me not to worry, that L.J. was with him and doing fine." The monsignor had died 10 years before.

That was not the first time JoAnn had seen that the dead communicate somehow via telephone. Her brother-in-law was in the Korean War when her mother-in-law answered her phone and heard her son Gaylord's voice, "Mom, I am okay. Don't worry about me." That was it. The phone call ended. A telegram came two days later – Gaylord had gone missing.

JoAnn said the date of April 8 was very significant: Aaron's Great-Grandma Schaffer[i] was born on an April 8, (4-8); his Great-Grandpa Schaffer (Gaylord's father) died on an April 8 (4-8). JoAnn's mother/Aaron's great-grandma was buried on an April 8 (4-8). We claimed 48 as the Schaffer number.

April 5: Kandy and I went to print Dad's "Baby Girl 2" picture. A young man named Joe came to help and I told him about the messages from Dad, Aniceto, and Aaron. Joe replied, "Absolutely. It happens all the time. People don't die and just leave. They stay. They are telling you they are here."

---

[i] Aaron's first home was with this Grandma. In the same house where the phone call from Gaylord had been received.

I then took Kandy to an appointment and went to wait for her at "Dad's library." I met a little boy named Orin, who repeated almost verbatim, Joe's words, "When people die, they don't just leave. They stay and they can make the phone ring." Orin knew more at seven than I knew at fifty-six.

May 15: Oh my GOD!!! I WON TWO READINGS FROM FOREVER FAMILY. Oh my God! The letter has the date of 2010. Aaron's year. (Instead of the actual year – 2011.)

June 5: Reading with Dave Campbell …

June 8: A friend of Alejo's told him that he wanted to recommend a psychologist who had helped him reach his mother after she had died. That is what he told Alejo. Her name is Rosa Elena and *she lives in this same building.*

June 10: Today I met Rosa Elena. She can help. I feel it. She is surrounded by joy. Her goal with her clients is to get them to KNOW FOR THEMSELVES that "dead people" are still here and that a relationship is possible. She says that Aaron is in the fourth dimension and that we are in the third. I don't know what that means, but she seems very sure.

She tells me that Aaron completed what he came to do and that I have not, and that *by working with him I will know what death means.*

I am working hard, but it is a long and mostly tortuous road. Sometimes I feel I will be able to understand, but at other times, I want to give up and die – I am so very tired. All day long, I snap my fingers, and repeat: "1, 2, 3 – *snap* – someone died. 1, 2, 3 – *snap* – someone died." It helps. I don't know why, but it does.

June 18: Rosa Elena tells me that I might want to consider participating in a "toma of Ayahuasca," which she calls a sacred plant with energy and consciousness properties. The group includes doctors, psychologists, and a couple whose little girl drowned at her 5th birthday party. It is scheduled for *JULY 2!* I am going to go. Alejo says he might come too.

June 22: The word *irascible* came so strongly to mind, I had to write it down in the dark. (Hypnagogia.)

We now go to November 8, 2013. This is Aaron's Grandpa Schaffer's birthday and one of the two feast days of Uriel, of which I am to be especially alert:

> A few of us were having breakfast following a mass for Aaron. Father Hurley, a long-time family friend, was talking to us about death's impact on families. When he mentioned "an *irascible* old fellow," I was immediately alert. I said aloud, to everyone, that I had heard *irascible* in hypnogogia and that I knew something important was in the air.[i]

> Father Hurley finished his story and said, "Well, I have to go now. I have an unusual task this afternoon. I am blessing a gravestone for a man who died in the Korean War 62 years ago. Don't know if he is related to Aaron; his name is Gaylord Schaffer."

The same Gaylord whose voice came through to his mother via telephone when he went missing in action in Korea, in the same house that was Aaron's first home. **CLICK.**

---

[i] The mass was celebrated at Saint Joseph's Catholic Church in Des Moines, where Aaron's funeral service had been held. The first time I had been in the church was in 1968, when I went to mass there with my friend Kathy to meet her cousin, Joe Schaffer. And meet him I did. In April of 1972, Joe and I were married by the same Father Hurley who had just used the word *irascible*. On July 24, 2010, the same Father Hurley held Aaron's memorial service in the same church where Aaron's parents had met 42 years earlier. Father Hurley had been transferred there two weeks earlier.

Reincarnation: Kim and I were at her house marveling over the *Gaylord-irascible-Father Hurley-St. Joseph's* connection when suddenly Kim exclaimed,

> "Cathy! This is so weird. It's like you were my great-grandmother standing there at the counter. Oh my God! This feels very strange."
> "What's her name?" I asked.
> "I have no idea," Kim replied.
> "Well, if it is Katarina, we'll know reincarnation[i] is true," I said without thinking.

Two weeks later Kim calls and says, "Guess what my Great-Grandma's name is. Katarina Brumm." Makes you wonder. Or at least it *could*.

June 30: Dream with Aaron: We were in a white pickup truck. Aaron was in the driver's seat. I tell him, "You can't drive, Aaron. You died." He said, "Wow, Mom, I didn't die. I just had a heart attack. You are taking this way too hard." And then he drove in reverse, VERY fast, out of that driveway.

July 1: Dream with Aaron: Aaron and I were at the Hy-Vee grocery store in Iowa City, having coffee and chatting away. I thought, "Well, this isn't so bad, if we can meet up like this."

---

[i] I knew nothing about reincarnation, but I had absorbed a few beliefs from my surrounding community. I was surprised to read about *Origen*, an early church father whose writings on reincarnation had been accepted and taught for a few centuries. His writings, along with so many other early Christian texts, were successfully labeled heresy. Reincarnation was deemed so offensive to Roman Emperor Justinian that he made the teaching of it a capital offense. I was even more surprised to learn that Pope Vigilius was jailed for refusing to sign the Emperor's decree. I began to realize that I, and most of those I knew, had unconsciously absorbed Justinian's decree, and had come to believe that "reincarnation is a heresy." When I read about physicist Erwin Schrodinger's model of *reincarnation as a logical consequence of equating space with consciousness*, I understood only enough to know that every time I say, "I don't believe in that," I am falling back into a habit that forbids knowing more.

July 2: The Ayahuasca encounter was on a small island on the Venezuelan Caribbean coast. There were about 30 of us. All ages, even kids, and with every occupation you can think of.

Someone came and asked me if my son had died. She said that a woman was seeing someone's dead son, who said to find his mom, who had very blue eyes, because he wanted her to know that he is okay. I went and the woman told me that my son was very worried about me. That I did not understand death, and that he was trying to help. Only Rosa Elena knew that Aaron had died.

The next morning, during the group discussions of the various experiences, Rosa Elena said that Aaron had come to her and asked her to tell me that he is okay, but that she had told him, "Don't manipulate me, Aaron. She wants to hear it from YOU." He replied, "But, look at her. I can't get to her. She is in too much pain." Rosa Elena said that she saw me as skeletal-like, weighing about 30 pounds less, with my face distorted with pain, so she said, "Okay Aaron, I'll tell her."

As for my experience with Ayahuasca[i], I didn't see Aaron. And GOD how I wanted to, but I did see all the stars connected to each other and felt everything and everyone webbed by some sort of force or gossamer threads.[ii] I felt that this part of life *is* beautiful and that it is worth living it.

---

[i] Research on Ayahuasca led me to Terrance and Dennis McKenna's work on the evolution of consciousness. This very quickly led me into the absolute realization of the truth of Montaigne's words, "Nothing is so firmly believed as that which we least know." It was shocking to become so aware of how I defended inherited beliefs as truth.

[ii] I wrote these words into my Walk-About Book and then looked up the word *gossamer* to read Walt Whitman's poem: A Noiseless Patient Spider. **CLICK. I FELT IT.**

Works Cited

*"Employ your time in improving yourself by other men's writings,
so that you shall gain easily what others have labored hard for."*
–Socrates

A Course in Miracles Combined Volume. Mill Valley: Foundation for Inner Peace, 2007.

Beichler, James. *To Die For: The Physical Reality of Conscious Survival*. Kindle Edition, 2013.

Bucke, Richard Maurice. *Cosmic Consciousness: A Study in the Evolution of the Human Mind*. Kindle Edition, 2013.

Campbell, Joseph. *The Hero with a Thousand Faces*. Republished by Princeton University Press, 2004.

Doyle, Arthur Conan. *The New Revelation*. Kindle Edition, 2011.

Eliade, Mircea. *The Sacred and the Profane*. Harcourt Brace & World, Inc., 1959.

Frankl, Viktor. *Man's Search for Meaning*. Republished by Beacon Press, 2006. ISBN: 978-0-8070-1429-5.

Freke, Timothy and Gandy, Peter. *The Laughing Jesus: Religious Lies and Gnostic Wisdom*. Harmony Books. 2005.

Goswami, Amit. *The Self-Aware Universe: How Consciousness Creates the Material World*. Penguin Putnam Inc, 1993.

Hilman, James and Shamdasani, Sonu. *Lament of the Dead: Psychology After Jung's Red Book*. Kindle Edition, 2013.

Holy Bible, King James Version, Red Letter Edition. Regency, 1978.

(The) I-Ching or Book of Changes. Bollingen Series XIX. Princeton University Press, 1950.

Jung, C.G. *Synchronicity: An Acausal Connecting Principle.* Princeton University Press, 2010.
_____*Psychology and Alchemy.* Collected Works of C.G. Jung. Volume 12. Republished by Princeton University Press, 1980. Kindle Digital Edition, 2014.

Lachman, Gary. *A Secret History of Consciousness.* Lindisfarne Books, 2003.

_____*Jung The Mystic: The Esoteric Dimensions of Carl Jung's Life and Teachings.* Jeremy P. Tarcher/Penguin, 2010.

Lehmann, Rosamond. *Swan in the Evening: Fragments of an Inner Life.* Little, Brown Book Group, 1982.

Lodge, Sir Oliver. *Raymond, Or Life and Death with Examples of the Evidence for Survival and Affection After Death.* Methuen & Co. LTD, 1916.

Marshall, Catherine. *To Live Again.* Avon Book, 1972.

Mitchell, Edgar, and Williams, Dwight. *The Way of the Explorer: An Apollo Astronaut's Journey Through the Material and Mystical Worlds.* The Career Press. 2008.

Philips, J.B. *The New Testament in Modern English.* Simon & Schuster, 1972.

Sendak, Maurice. *Where the Wild Things Are.* Harper & Row, 1963.

Schafer, Lothar. *Infinite Potential: What Quantum Physics Reveals about How We Should Live.* Kindle Edition. 2013.

Tart, Charles. *The End of Materialism: How Evidence of the Paranormal is Bringing Science and Spirit Together.* ISBN 978-1572246454) Kindle Edition, 2012.

Van Dusen, Wilson. *The Natural Depth in Man.* Kindle Edition, ISBN: 978-0-87785 692-4.

Wade, Jenny. *Changes of Mind: A Holonomic Theory of the Evolution of Consciousness.* State University of New York Press, 1996. Kindle Edition, 2010.

Wilhelm, Richard. Translation from Chinese into German of *The I-Ching or Book of Changes.* Rendered into English by Cary F. Baynes. Third Edition. Princeton University Press, 1967.

Wilson, Colin. The *Occult: A History.* Granada Publishing Limited, 1973.

End Notes

"I was amazed to find what a number of great men – men whose names were to the fore in science – thoroughly believed that spirit was independent of matter and could survive it."

–Arthur Conan Doyle

[1] billmoyers.com/content/ep-1-joseph-campbell-and-the-power-of-myth-the-hero's-adventure-audio. Accessed June 2016.

[2] Marshall, Catherine. *To Live Again*. Page 196.

[3] Ibid. Page 20.

[4] Permission for use granted by Eddison Books Ltd.

[5] https://kbachuntitled.files.wordpress.com/2013/04/rainer-maria-rilke-letters-to-a-young-poet.pdf. Accessed September 2017.

[6] VanDusen, Wilson. *The Natural Depth in Man*. Kindle Edition. Chapter 3. Section: To See and Hear Feeling. Paragraph 5.

[7] Tart, Charles T. *The End of Materialism: How Evidence of the Paranormal Is Bringing Science and Spirit Together*. Kindle Edition. Chapter 3. Section: Pathologies of Knowing and Learning. Paragraph 3.

[8] Ibid. Paragraph 6.

[9] Eliade, Mircea. *The Sacred and the Profane. The Nature of Religion: The significance of religious myth, symbolism, and ritual within life and culture*. Page 11.

[10] http://jungiancenter.org/jung-on-numbers/#_ftnref. Accessed December 2017.

[11] Schafer, Lothar. *Infinite Potential: What Quantum Physics Reveals About How We Should Live*. Kindle Edition. Introduction. The Power of Mathematical Forms. Paragraph 4.

[12] Jung, Carl. *Synchronicity. An Acausal Connecting Principle*. Collected Works. Volume 8. Bollingen Series XX. Page 102.

[13] Jung, Carl. www.iging.com/intro/foreword.htm. Accessed September 2017.

[14] Schäfer, Lothar. *Infinite Potential: What Quantum Physics Reveals About How We Should Live*. Kindle Edition, page 25.

[15] Frankl, Viktor. *Man's Search for Meaning*. Page 118.

[16] https://www.facebook.com/JosephCampbellFoundation/post s/111752255543862. Accessed September 2017.

[17] http://www.sprweb.org/ accessed September 2017.

[18] whitecrowbooks.com/michaeltymn/entry Section: Forever Family Foundation: Practical Bereavement, accessed September 2017.

[19] Van Dusen, Wilson. *The Natural Depth in Man*. Kindle Edition. Chapter 1. Section: The Castle of the Mind. Paragraph 5.

[20] Lachman, Gary. *A Secret History of Consciousness*. Page 144.

[21] Van Dusen, Wilson. The *Natural Depth in Man*. Kindle Edition. Chapter 7. Section: Fragile Fringe Phenomena. Paragraph 5.

[22] Bucke, Richard. Maurice. *Cosmic Consciousness: A Study in the Evolution of the Human Mind*. Kindle Edition. Chapter One. Section IV. Paragraph 3.

[23] Ibid. Section V. Paragraph 17.

[24] Mitchell, Edgar. *The Way of the Explorer: An Apollo Astronaut's Journey Through the Material and Mystical Worlds*. Pages 58-59.

[25] Wilson, Colin. *The Occult: A History*. Page 176.

[26] Lehmann, Rosamond. *Swan in the Evening: Fragments of an Inner Life*. Page 88.

[27] Jung, C.G.. From *Psychology and Alchemy*. The Collected Works. Volume 12. Kindle Digital Edition. Part I. Paragraph 2.

[28] Van Dusen, Wilson. *The Natural Depth in Man*. Kindle Edition. Section 1. Paragraph 5.

[28] Lachman, Gary. *A Secret History of Consciousness*. Page 257.

[29] Hilman, James and Shamdasani, Sonu. Kindle Edition. First Conversation. Paragraph 2.

[30] Ibid. Paragraph 8.

[31] Ibid. Paragraph 38.

[32] Ibid. Paragraph 39.